IN THE
beginning
GOD

— IN THE —
beginning
GOD

Second edition

HOMER C. HOEKSEMA

REFORMED
FREE PUBLISHING
ASSOCIATION
Jenison, Michigan

© 2015 Reformed Free Publishing Association

First edition 1966
Reprint 1974
Second edition 2015

Scripture cited is taken from the King James (Authorized) Version

Cover design by Zoran Opalic
Interior design by Katherine Lloyd, The DESK

Reformed Free Publishing Association
1894 Georgetown Center Drive
Jenison, Michigan 49428
616-457-5970
www.rfpa.org

ISBN 978-1-936054-76-3
ISBN ebook 978-1-936054-77-0
LCCN 2015933690

In the beginning God created the heaven and the earth.

And the earth was without form, and void; and darkness was upon the face of the deep. And the spirit of God moved upon the face of the waters. And God said, Let there be light: and there was light. And God saw the light, that it was good: and God divided the light from the darkness. And God called the light Day, and the darkness he called Night. And the evening and the morning were the first day.

And God said, Let there be a firmament in the midst of the waters, and let it divide the waters from the waters. And God made the firmament, and divided the waters which were under the firmament from the waters which were above the firmament: and it was so. And God called the firmament Heaven. And the evening and the morning were the second day.

And God said, Let the waters under the heaven be gathered together unto one place, and let the dry land appear: and it was so. And God called the dry land Earth; and the gathering together of the waters called he Seas: and God saw that it was good. And God said, Let the earth bring forth grass, the herb yielding seed, and the fruit tree yielding fruit after his kind, whose seed is in itself, upon the earth: and it was so. And the earth brought forth grass, and herb yielding seed after his kind, and the tree yielding fruit, whose seed was in itself, after his kind: and God saw that it was good. And the evening and the morning were the third day.

And God said, Let there be lights in the firmament of the heaven to divide the day from the night; and let them be for signs, and for seasons, and for days, and years: and let them be for lights in the firmament of the heaven to give light upon the earth: and it was so. And God made two great lights; the greater light to rule the day, and the lesser light to rule the night: he made the stars also. And God set them in the firmament of the heaven to give light upon the earth, and to rule over the day and over the night, and to divide the light from the darkness: and God saw that it was good. And the evening and the morning were the fourth day.

And God said, Let the waters bring forth abundantly the moving creature that hath life, and fowl that may fly above the earth in the open firmament of heaven. And God created great whales, and every living creature that moveth, which the waters brought forth abundantly, after their kind, and every winged fowl after his kind: and God saw that it was good. And God blessed them, saying, Be fruitful, and multiply, and fill the waters in the seas, and let fowl multiply in the earth. And the evening and the morning were the fifth day.

And God said, Let the earth bring forth the living creature after his kind, cattle, and creeping thing, and beast of the earth after his kind: and it was so. And God made the beast of the earth after his kind, and cattle after their kind, and every thing that creepeth upon the earth after his kind: and God saw that it was good. And God said, Let us make man in our image, after our likeness: and let them have dominion over the fish of the sea, and over the fowl of the air, and over the cattle, and over all the earth, and over every creeping thing that creepeth upon the earth. So God created man in his own image, in the image of God created he him; male and female created he them. And God saw everything that he had made, and, behold, it was very good. And the evening and the morning were the sixth day.

Thus the heavens and the earth were finished, and all the host of them. And on the seventh day God ended his work which he had made; and he rested on the seventh day from all his work which he had made. And God blessed the seventh day, and sanctified it: because that in it he had rested from all his work which God created and made.

And the LORD God said, It is not good that the man should be alone; I will make him an help meet for him. And out of the ground the LORD God formed every beast of the field, and every fowl of the air; and brought them unto Adam to see what he would call them: and whatsoever Adam called every living creature, that was the name thereof. And Adam gave names to all cattle, and to the fowl of the air, and to every beast of the field; but for Adam there was not found an help meet for him. And the LORD God caused a deep sleep to fall upon Adam, and he slept: and he took one of his ribs, and closed up the flesh instead thereof; and the rib, which the LORD God had taken from man, made he a woman, and brought her unto the man. And Adam said, This is now bone of my bones, and flesh of my flesh: she shall be called Woman, because she was taken out of Man.

—GENESIS 1:1–28, 31; 2:1–3, 18–23

*C*ontents

Foreword

Fifty years after it was initially published, the Reformed Free Publishing Association is pleased to offer this second edition of *In the Beginning God* by Homer C. Hoeksema.

The 1960s were years of challenges to the infallibility and authority of scripture. These attacks were precipitated by the increasingly popular theory of evolution, especially theistic evolution, which was making inroads into Reformed churches and schools, particularly into institutions of higher learning. In opposition to this creeping heresy and in unequivocal defense of the doctrine of scripture, Homer C. Hoeksema gave three public lectures and then put them into written form.

The reason for republishing this book is that the issue of evolution versus creation has not faded away, but has instead intensified. The doctrine of scripture has increasingly been compromised and denied, and evolutionism has increasingly dominated the teaching of allegedly Reformed schools. Rather than diminishing in significance, the importance of the conflict between creation and evolution has intensified. The denial of biblical creation in six, literal, twenty-four-hour days and the predominance of secular evolutionistic theories are reasons for being knowledgeable on these subjects, for maintaining the givens of the inspiration and authority of scripture, and thus for the republication of *In the Beginning God*.

In Christian educational institutions, historically other disciplines were viewed through the lens of theology, which was considered to be the queen of the sciences. In recent decades the reverse has become true: theology is viewed in the light of and is determined by other disciplines, notably the natural sciences.

In much of the Christian community the idea of an old universe has gained wider acceptance than it had some decades ago. Today theistic evolutionism is taught rigidly in most Christian institutions of higher learning. It is assumed to be true in the natural sciences and is taught in every discipline.

In contrast to the lie of evolution, the author sharply advocates and delineates the truth of divine creation in six days as taught in scripture. He uncompromisingly makes clear that the central issue between creation and evolution is one of faith versus unbelief.

The RFPA echoes the author's sentiment in his preface: "It is my hope and prayer that these pages may be instructive, and that they may serve to strengthen the resolve of God's children to hold fast to the truth and to call many who have departed or who are departing back to the old paths."

Mark H. Hoeksema

Preface

$\mathcal{T}$he three chapters of this little book were originally three lectures delivered during the winter and
spring of 1966 at the First Protestant Reformed Church
of Grand Rapids, Michigan. The purpose of these lectures was to give a clear exposition and defense of a
precious truth of our Reformed heritage that is under fre-
quent attack in our times, the truth of creation as set forth
by scripture. Because of the gratifying response from the
large audiences that attended these lectures, and because
of numerous requests for printed copies, also from many
who were not able to attend these lectures, it was decided to
publish them.

A spoken message, however, loses something of its
effect when it is put on the dead page. For this reason, and
because publication gave me the opportunity to expand
several thoughts that I had no time to develop when I

lectured, these chapters, while basically the same as the lectures, are slightly different in form and in length.

It is my hope and prayer that these pages will be instructive and that they will serve to strengthen the resolve of God's children to hold fast to the truth and to call many who have departed or are departing back to the old paths.

Homer C. Hoeksema
June, 1966

Chapter 1

THE DIVINE FOUNDATION— THE INFALLIBLE SCRIPTURES

*T*he subject of the infallible scriptures is almost everywhere today the subject of discussion and a large measure of controversy in the churches. The inspired scriptures are the center of much attack, and so this subject can be said to be a current issue and one of concern to those who would keep the faith once delivered to the saints.

Let me mention some examples.

There is out-and-out modernism, which always attacks the scriptures and has no use for holy scripture whatsoever. That spirit of modernism has arisen especially since the eighteenth and nineteenth centuries. With this modernism we are not concerned, for with respect to it the lines of demarcation have been drawn long ago.

There is new modernism, sometimes called neo-orthodoxy, which is represented by Karl Barth and Emil Brunner and the demythologizing school of Rudolph Bultmann. New modernism also attacks the scriptures and does not recognize them as infallible. The more one investigates new modernism, the more one discovers that it is not new at all, but is essentially the same old modernism. My concern is that this theology, with its denial of the scriptures, has found its way in more than one instance into orthodox areas and even into Reformed churches. Therefore its influence must be guarded against.

There has also been considerable discussion regarding the scriptures in connection with the recent Vatican Council. There have been those who look in vain for signs that Rome will return to the principle of the absolute and sole authority of holy scripture.

Coming a little nearer to the Reformed, among Lutherans the subject of holy scripture is very much an issue. Scripture is under attack particularly among those Lutherans who are classified as orthodox (for example, the Missouri Synod). There is no little degree of stress and strain and even separation in that denomination because of the issue of the infallible scriptures.

In Presbyterian churches also the scriptures have been under attack for a long time. The Orthodox Presbyterian Church, for example, had its origin in part because of the liberal denial of the scriptures and of their absolute authority that was rampant in the parent denomination. Still today the issue to some extent is a live one in Presbyterianism. Witness the attempt to set aside completely the Westminster Confession in the Confession of 1967 that is being proposed in the United Presbyterian Church.

Still nearer to the Reformed faith, today one finds similar symptoms in the Protestant church in the Netherlands. In the Reformed Churches (*Gereformeerde Kerken*) of the Netherlands[1] the movement has gained ground to set aside the decisions of the Synod of Assen in the case

---

[1] This denomination has since merged with other churches to form the present *Protestantse Kerk in Nederland* (PKN).

that involved Peter Geelkerken in 1926 and that was concerned with the first three chapters of Genesis and with those articles of the Belgic Confession that deal with the infallibility and authority of holy scripture. This is an example of the ecclesiastical stress and strain connected with the matter of scripture's infallibility and authority.

Also in Reformed circles in the United States there are phenomena of this kind. The Reformed Church in America has had it difficulties with the nature of the scriptures. Particularly in New Brunswick Seminary liberal tendencies regarding holy scripture have arisen. For example, scripture was the basic issue in the case a few years ago that involved the historicity of the first part of the book of Genesis. I have no doubt that somewhere, buried not too deeply among the issues, this same issue of holy scripture is involved in the merger proposal between the Reformed Church in America and the Southern Presbyterian Church.

The same phenomena are found in the Christian Reformed Church in the United States. In the 1920s there was the Janssen case, which involved essentially this same issue concerning holy scripture. In the 1930s there was the lesser known Wezeman case, which also involved

4

the issues of higher criticism. Just a few years ago there was the flurry that resulted in a report on infallibility and the decision to commend this report to the churches.

Today there is much discussion in various churches centering on questions involving the book of Genesis, and especially the truth of creation is coming under discussion. Essentially all of these discussions involve the inspiration, infallibility, and authority of holy scripture.

I mention these examples for two reasons. First, I want to show how current and widespread this issue regarding holy scripture is at present. Various attacks on holy scripture are a common phenomenon even in churches that are generally classified as orthodox. Second, I mention these various examples to point out that in almost all of these cases that center on holy scripture the one common element concerns Genesis, creation, theistic evolution, the historical reality of the fall, and the alleged scientific findings and evidence concerning the age of the earth and evolution. In order to discuss the subject of creation, together with the related issues concerning the book of Genesis, it is essential to have a clear understanding of the truth of the infallibility of scripture.

It is not my purpose to throw barbs at any particular group of churches or at anyone's church, or to reproach anyone personally. I have no interest in that whatsoever. The subjects of the inspiration, infallibility, and authority of scripture and of the doctrine of creation are far too serious and important to use them for such a purpose. I will be critical, and I will be concretely critical of various positions that are held. But my purpose is to clarify the issues, to remind you of the truth that has always been Reformed, and to sound a warning, because these truths are of the utmost importance to the church.

I also will not attempt to furnish a long discourse, proof, and argumentation on inspiration and infallibility. That will take us too far afield and will needlessly lengthen this discussion. Rather, I will set forth briefly and pointedly the truth as the Reformed faith and the churches of the Reformation have always maintained it. Further, I will demonstrate the importance of this truth for the entire structure of the truth and of the faith of the church and point out the practical significance of all this for us as members of Christ's church who seek and love the truth.

The Truth That the Scriptures Are Inspired and Infallible

The subject is the scriptures, the sixty-six books of the Old and New Testaments, commonly called the canon of holy scripture. I do not intend to discuss that canon *per se* and the formation of the canon, but to proceed on the basis that these books are the canon of holy scripture and that the apocryphal books are excluded from this discussion. This mention of the term *canon* provides an occasion to point to the importance of this subject. *Canon* means "measuring rod" and therefore "standard, criterion, rule." In connection with this term the well–known expression (almost a model of the Reformation) has arisen, namely, that the scriptures are our only infallible rule of faith and life or of doctrine and practice.

When referring to the scriptures, I mean the scriptures as they were originally written: the autographs, as they are called. We no longer have those autographs. There are in the original languages only thousands of copies and partial copies of the scriptures. The documents as the prophets and apostles wrote them are providentially not

7

in existence today. The principle of infallibility applies, strictly speaking, to those original documents. Nevertheless, this does not mean that the infallibility of scripture has no meaning for us today. While we do not have the autographs, that makes no real difference for several reasons. Although there are literally thousands of variations in the readings of scripture in the various manuscripts or copies that have been discovered, in these many thousands of variations there is not one in which an article of faith is in jeopardy. Among those thousands of variations in readings there is only a small fraction that is of any significance for the meaning of the text and for the meaning of holy scripture. In our time the biblical science of textual criticism (not to be confused with unbelieving higher criticism)—the science that is concerned with the correct reading of a certain passage from among the various readings—has been very highly developed, so that even with all these variations our Bible is today very accurate. Even scripture itself does not consider the lack of these autographs as a serious obstacle. In the apostle Paul's time Timothy certainly did not possess the autographs of the Old Testament scriptures, in which he had been trained from his childhood. They were gone. Yet in 2 Timothy 3:16 Paul does not hesitate to say concerning those scriptures as Timothy possessed them and had been instructed in them, "All scripture is given by inspiration of God." This also applies to the scriptures as they are mentioned in 2 Peter 1:19–21:

> 19. We have also a more sure word of prophecy; whereunto ye do well that ye take heed, as unto a light that shineth in a dark place, until the day dawn, and the day star arise in your hearts.
> 20. Knowing this first, that no prophecy of the scripture is of any private interpretation.
> 21. For the prophecy came not in old time by the will of man: but holy men of God spake as they were moved by the Holy Ghost.

The scriptures as we have them are the written record of the word of God. This is a great wonder. From among all books and all writings you can single out the scriptures and say about them, "This book is the word of God himself." Revelation—that God speaks and makes known his word in earthly, human language on our level—is a wonder. Inspiration—that God caused holy men to speak and to write his word—is also a tremendous wonder.

This is important practically with respect to inspiration, infallibility, and the various problems and questions that arise in connection with these truths. I fear that we are sometimes inclined to forget this. When we do forget, we are inclined to take a rationalistic approach and attempt to meet the opponent of the scriptures and of infallibility on his rationalistic ground. When we cannot succeed in overcoming his apparently well-reasoned arguments, we weaken and begin to have doubts concerning inspiration and infallibility, and we become inclined to compromise.

Hence we must remember that the Bible and its inspiration and its infallibility are strictly matters of faith. This means that the truth of infallibility is a spiritual matter: not a matter of the head, but a matter of the heart. The unbeliever cannot recognize the Bible as the inspired and infallible word of God. That is a matter of the heart, a matter of faith. We stand on holy ground when we talk about scripture, and we ought to be deeply aware of this. Faith does not start with the question, is the Bible the word of God? Faith starts with the proposition that the Bible *is* the word of God. All the questions and problems that may arise and must be faced in connection with the Bible—and there are undeniably many of them, including many apparent conflicts that we cannot reconcile—must be considered and discussed within the confines of the conviction that the Bible is the word of God. That means that they must always be considered and discussed in reverent fear of God. The Bible as the word of God in its divinely inspired and infallible character towers far above any human, sinful efforts to contradict the Bible, and it towers above any merely human efforts to defend it. The truth of the Bible depends on neither. It depends on God. God's word and its truth are not dependent on our understanding, but our understanding is dependent on the word of God.

What is inspiration? Inspiration is the wonder of God's grace whereby holy men were so moved by the Holy Spirit that what they spoke and wrote was the word of God.

This truth of inspiration has come under attack. These attacks have arisen primarily since the Reformation and since the confessions were written. The Reformation was concerned with the truth of scripture, but its concern was mostly about the absolute or sole authority of holy scripture in contradiction of Rome, which recognized sources of authority other than and next to scripture. After the Reformation the attacks on holy scripture took on a different form, that of attacks on the inspiration and the infallibility of scripture. In such attacks the authority of scripture was vulnerable. When the Reformation had returned to the principle of the sole authority of scripture, that authority came under attack by way of attacks on its inspired character and infallibility.

Against these attacks various terms came into use that further describe and define the truth of inspiration. These terms are *graphic, plenary, verbal,* and *organic.*

Graphic, Plenary, and Verbal Inspiration

First is the term *graphic inspiration.* The term *graphic* comes from a root that means "to write," and the expression graphic inspiration simply means that the Holy Spirit inspired and moved holy men to write the word of God.

Men not only spoke the word of God, but they also wrote the word of God.

Second, although the term *graphic* is sufficient in itself, because of attacks it proved to be insufficient. It was not enough to say only that men were moved by the Holy Spirit to write the word of God. Another term came into use as a description of inspiration, a term designed to make the meaning of inspiration more explicit. That term is *plenary*. Plenary inspiration means that the Bible is fully inspired, totally inspired, inspired in all its parts. This limitation is designed to make it impossible for men to say they believe the truth of inspiration and at the same time to deny that the Bible is in its entirety the written record of God's word. It is designed to make it impossible for anyone to say that the word of God is only *in* the Bible, so that parts of the Bible are the word of God and parts of it are not the word of God. Plenary inspiration insists that the Bible is from beginning to end the written record of the word of God, the word of God in all its parts. One cannot go through the Bible picking and choosing what part is the word of God and what part is not the word of God, or deciding that one part is inspired and infallible while another part is not inspired and infallible. It is all or nothing.

The third term is *verbal inspiration*. This term also has become necessary because there were and are those who despite the term *plenary inspiration* wanted to say that while the *thoughts* of the Bible were inspired, the expression of those thoughts, the language and the words in which those thoughts were conveyed, was not inspired. The expression of the thoughts, the language, was left to human writers and is fallible. There is no room for any such idea in the concept of inspiration, and especially not in the idea of plenary inspiration. It is inconceivable and utterly inconsistent to make such a separation between thoughts and words. Because men have repeatedly attempted to make that distinction, it became necessary to use the term *verbal*. Verbal inspiration emphasizes that inspiration is such that the Bible in its expressions, words, and language is completely the word of God.

Organic Inspiration

Finally, the term *organic inspiration* has arisen, chiefly because there were those who ridiculed the idea of verbal inspiration as a "dictation theory." This ridicule claims that the whole concept of plenary and verbal inspiration makes of the holy men who wrote the Bible nothing but secretaries and stenographers. That is a wicked ridicule, for there have been no churches and no theologians of note who have at any time adhered rigidly to a strict dictation theory, even though they may have employed the term *dictation*. John Calvin used the term *dictation*, but he did not believe in any dictation theory. At least in part, the rise of this ridiculing criticism accounts for the use of the term *organic inspiration*.

Organic inspiration means that the Bible is an organism, that it is one, that it has one principle, one center, Christ, and that all its books and writings have their central principle or their root in Christ. The Bible is the word of God in Christ. Essentially the whole content of the word of God is revealed in the protevangel, the great mother promise of Genesis 3:15: "I will put enmity between thee and the woman, and between thy seed and her seed; it shall bruise thy head, and thou shalt bruise his heel." The rest of scripture is nothing else than a further elucidation and an ever clearer and brighter revelation of that promise first given in paradise. All of scripture grows out of that one promise.

We are interested in the meaning of this organic conception with respect to inspiration and the method of inspiration.

First, just as God conceived sovereignly and from eternity of his people as an organism in Christ, so he conceived in his eternal counsel of the whole of scripture as one organism as a revelation of himself in Christ Jesus, the heart of that entire revelation. The Bible that was written over the course of many centuries, in many different places and by many different men under many different circumstances, did not come into being by accident, nor was it mechanically put together either by God or by men. God planned holy scripture before the foundation of the world in such a way that all of its parts would arise out of and reveal one principle and one idea: the word of God in Christ. Each book and each part occupies its own place and serves in its own particular way in the whole of the word of God, which was not fully revealed until John wrote the book of Revelation.

Second, organic inspiration means that from eternity

God sovereignly conceived of and ordained special organs of Christ's body to be organs of inspiration to write his word. God ordained them *entirely*. It is not true that the Holy Spirit had a certain book and a certain purpose in mind and that he went about searching for the proper man to write that book. The Holy Spirit did not merely find and use men to write his scriptures. They were planned from before the foundation of the world. Their personalities, their characters, their talents, their experiences, their times, and their historical circumstances were so planned and designed from before the foundation of the world that each one of those men would be a fit instrument to write a certain part of God's word and to have a place in the writing of the whole of scripture.

Third, the Holy Spirit as the Spirit of Christ in time called, prepared, formed, and fitted these divinely ordained organs of inspiration for their divinely ordained tasks. Isaiah could not have prophesied as he did unless he was Isaiah, with his peculiar character and place in history. John could not have written his epistles in exactly the same form and style in which he wrote them unless God had made John exactly what he was. All this was included in the purpose and work of God with a view to the inscripturation of his word.

Fourth, the Spirit inspired holy men: he moved, carried, illumined, and guided them to write infallibly the word of the revelation of God in Christ. Hence men spoke and wrote entirely in harmony with their peculiar personalities, styles, circumstances, experiences, and times. But when they spoke and wrote, the product was not the word of man but the word of God.

The Infallible Scriptures

When you take all those various aspects of inspiration together, the result is the infallible scriptures, the inerrant, written word of God.

Inerrant and *infallible* are also terms that have arisen out of controversy regarding holy scripture. These terms have been occasioned by opposition to and denial of the truth of scripture. Essentially it is unnecessary to say that scripture is infallible, and historically it was not always necessary to say this. You could simply say, "Scripture is the word of God. Period!" But because of denials it became necessary to emphasize this truth over against the errors. On account of errors and denials of the truth it became necessary to make *explicit* what is *implicit* in the fact that the Bible is the word of God. A fallible and errant word of God is nothing but a contradiction in terms. A fallible Bible means that God errs, that God lies, that God make mistakes, that God's speech is inaccurate. This truth is simple: as soon as you maintain that the Bible is the word of God, and at the same time try to maintain that the Bible is fallible, you have a contradiction. In order to maintain that scripture is in any sense fallible, one must get rid of the idea that the Bible is the word of God or accuse God of fallibility. Thus the terms *infallible* and *inerrant* have come into use to emphasize the truth over against the errors. *Inerrant* means "not erring" or "without error." *Infallible* is the stronger term; it means "not capable of error."

Applied to the scriptures, these terms mean that the Bible as the written record of the word of God is altogether free from and incapable of error, inaccuracy, mistake, contradiction, and conflict. It is altogether the word of God, who cannot lie and who cannot make a mistake.

Here is the proper place to emphasize that this is a matter of faith. That scripture is infallible is true whether or not we can demonstrate this. Our belief in the infallibility of that word does not depend upon our understanding and our solving whatever problems may arise in our study of scripture. It does not depend on our ability to answer and to solve various questions and apparent contradictions and conflicts to which men may point. We must not take that approach. We must not question whether the Bible is the word of God and whether or not it is infallible. Faith begins from the position that scripture is the infallible word of God.

Scriptural Proof

That scripture is the infallible word of God is the Reformed position. It always has been the Reformed position, and it is the Reformed position today. It is the Reformed position because it is the truth of scripture.

I do not intend to argue that point or reason about it at length.

Scripture, however, speaks to the matter of inspiration.

In 2 Timothy 3:16 we read: "All scripture is given by inspiration of God, and is profitable for doctrine, for reproof, for correction, for instruction in righteousness." The Greek term translated as "given by inspiration of God" is literally "God-breathed." All scripture is God-breathed. That is a beautiful idea. It means that God breathed, and the Bible resulted. That is inspiration. Notice that this passage does not so much as mention men or the activity of men. They are not in the picture. Only this: "All scripture is God-breathed."

There is also the scriptural proof in 2 Peter 1:19–21:

19. We have also a more sure word of prophecy; whereunto ye do well that ye take heed, as unto a light that shineth in a dark place, until the day dawn, and the day star arise in your hearts:

20. Knowing this first, that no prophecy of the scripture is of any private interpretation.

21. For the prophecy came not in old time by the will of man: but holy men of God spake as they were moved by the Holy Ghost.

In these verses the human writers are mentioned. But what does the text say about them? "No prophecy of the scripture is of any private interpretation. For the prophecy came not in old time by the will of man." That is negative: it came *not* by the will of man. These men certainly did not write in spite of their own wills or against their wills. Yet the Bible that they wrote was not the product of the will of man, but holy men of God spoke as they were moved by the Holy Spirit.

In John 10:35 Jesus says, "The scripture cannot be broken." In his conversation with the Jews this statement is the foundation of Jesus' argument. If the scripture could be broken, Jesus' argument on the basis of Psalm 82 would fall away and be of no authority. But it is authoritative because "the scripture cannot be broken." Its authority is absolute and unimpeachable because it is divine and infallible.

John 5:45–47 assumes inerrancy and therefore absolute authority with respect to the writings of Moses:

45. Do not think that I will accuse you to the Father: there is one that accuseth you, even Moses, in whom ye trust.

46. For had ye believed Moses, ye would have believed me: for he wrote of me.

47. But if ye believe not his writings, how shall ye believe my words?

Plainly, according to this passage, if you do not believe Moses (that is, if you do not believe the Old Testament), you do not believe Christ. Vice versa, if you do not believe Christ, you do not believe Moses. The two are inseparable. Therefore the denial of the inspired and infallible character of the Old Testament scriptures is contrary to faith in Christ.

The Belgic Confession

The truth of the inspiration and infallibility of scripture is the current thought of the Belgic Confession, which speaks of scripture in articles 3–7. You will not find there the terms *graphic*, *verbal*, *plenary*, and *organic*. For the most part the use of these terms was not necessary at the time the Confession was written. But in it there are several noteworthy and clear expressions with respect to the scriptures.

Article 3 emphasizes strongly and without any limitation or qualification that the scriptures are the word of God:

> We confess that this Word of God was not sent, nor delivered by the will of man, but that *holy men of God spake as they were moved by the Holy Ghost*, as the Apostle Peter saith. And that afterwards God, from a special care which he has for us and our salvation, commanded his servants, the Prophets and Apostles, to commit his revealed Word to writing; and he himself wrote with his own finger the two tables of the law. Therefore we call such writings holy and divine Scriptures.[2]

Article 4 lists the canonical books. There is a significant statement in this article: "We believe that the Holy Scriptures are contained in two books, namely, the Old and New Testaments, which are canonical, against which

---

2 Belgic Confession 3, in Philip Schaff, ed., *The Creeds of Christendom with a History and Critical Notes*, 6th ed., 3 vols. (Harper and Rowe, 1931; repr., Grand Rapids, MI: Baker Book House, 2007), 3:384–85.

nothing can be alleged."[3] The point is that if there were error in these books, you could allege something against them and challenge the rightful place of such errant books in the canon of holy scripture. But they are inerrant and infallible. You can allege nothing against them.

In article 5 there is a significant statement that presupposes infallibility and freedom from error: "We receive all these books, and these only, as holy and canonical, for the regulation, foundation and confirmation of our faith; believing, without any doubt, all things contained in them."[4] This implies that they are free from error. If these books were known to be fallible and known to contain error, you could never confess to believe all things contained therein. Note that "all things" occurs without any limitation.

Article 6 indirectly teaches the same idea when it speaks of the difference between the canonical and the apocryphal books. This article sets up the canonical books as the absolute standard of authority in contrast

---

3 Belgic Confession 4, in ibid., 3:385.
4 Belgic Confession 5, in ibid.

to the apocryphal books. The church may "read and take instruction from" the apocryphal books "insofar as they agree with the canonical books." The apocryphal books can never "detract from the authority of the other sacred books."[5] This absolute authority of the canonical books again presupposes their infallibility.

Article 7, which speaks of the sufficiency of scripture, contains the statement: "Therefore we reject with all our hearts, whatsoever does not agree with this infallible rule, which the Apostles have taught us, saying, *Try the spirits whether they are of God*; likewise, *If there come any unto you, and bring not this doctrine, receive him not into your house.*"[6]

The Divine Foundation

All of the truths mentioned above constitute the divine foundation of the church.

In connection with the above statement, I refer you to scripture itself. The scriptures speak of their own

---

5 Belgic Confession 6, in ibid., 3:387

6 Belgic Confession 7, in ibid., 3:388–89.

importance for the whole structure of the truth in Ephesians 2:19–20: "Now therefore ye are no more strangers and foreigners, but fellow citizens with the saints, and of the household of God; and are built upon the foundation of the apostles and prophets, Jesus Christ himself being the chief corner stone." This passage refers to the apostles and prophets not as persons, because in that sense they are dead and in the grave, but to their teaching and preaching. It refers to the word of God by them as that word of God has as its chief and determining content, its cornerstone, Jesus Christ, the Word made flesh. That is the foundation on which the church, the household of God, the temple of God, is built. Hence the word of God, the scriptures, can rightly be called the foundation of the church.

A foundation is of the utmost importance to any building because it determines its shape, size, outline, and strength. You cannot build an Empire State Building, for example, on the foundation of a two-stall garage. It will not fit and will not hold up such a building. Ephesians 2 uses the figure of the foundation as the determining factor of a building with respect to the church as the spiritual building of God, in which he dwells and has fellowship with his people. We may conclude from this that the whole belief, the whole confession, the whole doctrine, the whole manner of life, and the entire manifestation of the church are built upon the word of God. Its divine foundation is the word of God as it has its infallible written record in all of the scriptures.

Here is the principle of the absolute authority of scripture. God's church is built on that foundation. It is the only foundation on which the church can be built. That foundation determines the building, and anything built on any other foundation cannot be built as the church. If you are not on the determining foundation for the whole church, then your building, whatever else it may be, cannot be the church. In order to be recognized as being of the church, any confession, belief, doctrine, or manner of life must be founded on scripture.

This fact is important from the viewpoint of the significance of that foundation and attacks on its divine character, authority, and infallibility. When you begin to chip away and to hammer away at the scriptures, you chip away at the foundation of the church.

Essentially that foundation cannot be destroyed. No one has ever destroyed it yet, and no one will ever destroy it. The foundation of God stands. However, in the practice and the confession of a church, of a denomination of churches, or of a member of the church, it is possible to chip away at the foundation and to deny the divine authority and strength of that foundation. This means that ultimately such a church, denomination of churches, or church member will stand on a different foundation, not on God's foundation.

But to cling to the figure, if you knock out a whole wall of a foundation, the building is not going to stand. It will tumble and crumble. The same is true of the scriptures. When you chip away at them, you are chipping away at the foundation of the church. This may seem insignificant at first, just as you can begin to destroy the foundation of a building by knocking a little chip out of one block in the wall. In fact, that has usually been the way the foundation of the scriptures has been attacked: just a little chip knocked off. If you keep on chipping, after a while an entire block goes out of the foundation; then the whole wall goes out; and finally the entire foundation is gone. If the foundation is destroyed, the entire building topples. If the strength of the foundation is destroyed, the strength of the building is gone too. You cannot build the church on any other foundation than the divinely appointed and constructed foundation of the scriptures.

That is why the truth of the infallibility of scripture is so serious: it concerns the foundation of the church.

Attacks on the Foundation

Today attacks are being made on that foundation. This has been done in the past, and it is being done today in many ways. Many are chipping away at the foundation.

There is the totally inconsistent idea of thought inspiration in distinction from word inspiration. According to this conception there are parts of scripture that are not the word of God, or there are parts that are erroneously, inaccurately, or imperfectly recorded and presented.

There is also the conception of two factors in the Bible: a divine factor and a human factor. I think that this expression of two factors is sometimes used with good intentions, but it is a dangerous expression. The Bible is the word of God, produced by one factor: divine inspiration. To the extent that you speak of a human factor, you must also speak of a human word.

The same is true of another distinction that is sometimes used with good intentions: a primary author (God) and secondary authors (men). The trouble with this distinction is that no matter how mightily you strive to distinguish between the primary and the secondary authors, you are still saying men are authors. They are not. The author of the scriptures is God. It is his word. It came not by the will of man, but by the will of God.

Another method of attack denies the historicity and the historical accuracy of various parts of the Bible and covers that up by calling such parts of scripture figurative, allegorical, or mythical. The most serious aspect of this attack is not that it denies the historicity of a certain passage of scripture, which is bad enough, but basically it attacks the authority and infallibility of scripture itself.

The same is true of the distinction that the Bible is accurate in its revelational purpose and sacred history, but that it can be inaccurate in peripheral matters and in mere history and historiography (the writing of history).

It is at this point that the weakness of the Report on Infallibility, commended to the churches in 1961 by the synod of the Christian Reformed Church, is glaring. That report was essentially a compromise. It failed to settle the most crucial issue in the whole discussion that occasioned it. It left room. A plain instance of this is seen in M. Hoogland's claim that the report leaves room for historical inaccuracies in scripture. In his article he gives a detailed analysis of this report in which he asserts that the report leaves room for maintaining that there is a sense in which it can be said that scripture is inaccurate. The following paragraph is an example:

> The report, therefore, supports the conclusion that it is possible to look at inaccuracy from more than one viewpoint, and consequently that it is possible to speak of historical inaccuracy while at the same time maintaining Scriptural accuracy in terms of sacred history. That is, what is seen as inaccurate from a merely historical viewpoint is recognized as wholly accurate for the reporting of sacred history. This conclusion being established by the

report and the report serving as the larger context in which the synodical declaration of 1959 must be seen (190), it becomes evident that the "actual historical inaccuracies" ruled out by the Synod of 1959 has reference to historical inaccuracies from the viewpoint of sacred history and not from the viewpoint of modern historiography.[7]

No one challenged the above statement or the article in which it appeared. The sad part is that the whole issue seems, at least for the present, to be buried in silence. That is a bad thing. I predict that in some form or other the same issue of scripture's infallibility is going to arise again because basically it was not settled.

The above are some of the implications of this foundation-idea and some of the methods of attack on the foundation.

All these devices have in common that they exalt man's subjective judgment above the word of God. Man decides

---

7 Marvin Hoogland, "Infallibility," *Reformed Journal* 11, no. 10 (November, 1961): 9–12.

what is and is not the word of God, what is accurate and what is inaccurate, and what is truth and what is error. This can be done with regard to relatively insignificant things at first; it often begins that way. That has been the history of every attack on the authority of scripture, but the principle is the important thing. When you begin to follow this method and this principle, essentially you have sacrificed the whole truth of infallibility. If you do not backtrack and return to the strict principle of infallibility, that error will blossom and have dire effects in time to come. That also is history.

Hence that divine foundation must always be built on. Every thought must be in submission to the scriptures, the only infallible rule. All our doctrine and all our life must conform to that rule, for it is the absolute authority. We must not come with outside evidences, philosophy, and science and try to make scripture conform to them. It is the other way around. This principle is important for all the truth and life of the church, but particularly for the wide-ranging discussions and questions concerning creation, the flood, evolution, and the age of the world. The truth regarding them must be decided solely in the light of and on the basis of scripture. Especially to some of those questions we will give our attention in the next two chapters, but that must be done on the basis of the position taken in this chapter.

Our Calling to Guard the Foundation

We must guard that foundation.

We must never allow anyone to chip away at it. If this is allowed, soon nothing will be left. The large denominations today that have departed completely from the infallible scriptures began by chipping. You cannot compromise regarding scripture. You cannot allow yourself to compromise by standing side by side in the same church communion and acting as though you are standing on the same basis with men who do deny or compromise this truth of scripture. That is an inconsistent position. If you do that, you lose your ability to fight for the maintenance of the truth.

We must adhere strictly to this as churches—in our doctrine, in our confession, in our teaching and preaching.

That is important for the preaching. This means that

the preaching that comes from any pulpit of a church that holds to the infallible scriptures must be expository. Its content must be the word of God. Preaching must not be topical and on the social issues of the day, as is so common today, even in Reformed churches. The scriptures must be expounded. This is important because the preaching of the word is the strength of the church. The preaching must never depart from the foundation of the scriptures.

As individual members of the church, we must all adhere to this principle. We must be on guard in this respect. Young men and young women, and especially young people of intellectual inclination—who can easily be flattered that they are intellectuals and who can have their egos tickled by the idea that they can learn something from philosophy and science over against scripture—must be on guard. One of the favorite ways of the devil is to attack the faith of young people with respect to the word of God. Hold, therefore, to the word of God as infallible in your personal faith, as members of the church.

This also includes the calling to speak out on the

doctrine of scripture. You must speak out on it not only in discussion and in writing. That is good; but ultimately, if nothing more is done, that will do no good. If the scriptures are attacked, speak out officially. Speak out ecclesiastically. Whether such protest looks hopeful or hopeless makes no difference. It is your right and calling as members of the church, as children of the Reformation, to speak out in the church. You must speak out, or ultimately you will lose the principle of infallibility by default.

Therefore let us hold to these scriptures. We cannot stand on two different foundations. We cannot stand on a half foundation. We cannot stand with those who attack the foundation. We must be uncompromising.

The Protestant Reformed Churches, who stand on the basis I have outlined above, pledge help and support, and if need be, shelter to anyone who wants to stand foursquare on that foundation, the only foundation on which the church may stand.

Chapter 2

THE CREATION RECORD–
LITERAL OR NOT LITERAL?

*T*he title of this chapter is in question form, which requires a word of explanation.

The alternatives posed could suggest that the creation record is an open question, a matter that is in doubt, and that we are about to conduct an investigation to determine whether or not we can arrive at a firm answer, and whether that answer must be that the creation record is to be literally or nonliterally understood. This is not an open question. It is my position that there is only one possible sense in which the creation record must be understood, and that the one sense is the literal sense. If I were to phrase the title of this chapter declaratively, I would phrase it this way: The Creation Record: Strictly Literal.

Why then is this question form employed? And why is this particular question asked?

The first reason is that there is currently much discussion and questioning about the subject of creation and the creation record. How is it to be understood? What does it mean? Does it allow room for any theory of evolution? Can the findings of science be harmonized with the account of creation? How are we to understand the days of creation week? These and many related questions are being raised currently. Besides, in many quarters there is a growing tendency to depart from positions that were formerly held with respect to the subject of creation. Anyone who follows the religious press is acquainted with this fact. Also in the Reformed community, both in this country and in the Netherlands, this subject is getting much attention. Therefore I feel that this question addresses an important issue that confronts the churches today.

Second, I chose this formulation because it states the basic issue in the entire discussion about creation. That discussion must come down to the question of the creation record as it is set forth by the Bible, particularly in the first part of the book of Genesis. There may be many other questions raised, and those questions may be either legitimate or improper. But the deepest questions are, what does the Bible say, and how does your presentation of creation harmonize with scripture? These are the unavoidable questions for the Bible-believing church and for the Bible-believing child of God. For that reason this chapter discusses scripture's account of creation.

Third, the question whether the creation record is literal or not accurately expresses the fundamental issue in the entire discussion of creation and the creation record.

I will proceed on the basis that the foundation of this chapter was laid in chapter I. The infallible scriptures are the only possible basis on which the church and the individual child of God can stand and dare to stand in dealing with any phase of the truth. That is a general principle. The scriptures, infallible from beginning to end, constitute the foundation of the entire structure of the truth. The truth of the infallibility and inerrancy of scripture comes into sharp focus particularly with respect to the truth of creation and the issues of creation versus evolution and of creation versus theistic evolution as explanations of the origin of the world, and the relation between creation and science's claims. Scripture's authority has become an unavoidable issue in the discussion concerning creation.

Whether one admits this or not, the denial of creation ultimately involves the denial of scripture. Hence scripture as the written word of God, from Genesis to Revelation, as absolutely infallible, is the basis for believers. The scriptures constitute the sole and absolute authority to which believers must appeal regarding the subject under discussion. The scriptures constitute the sole authority in all things. I emphasize that with respect to the subjects discussed in this chapter and the next one. It is necessary that we do not allow other authorities next to scripture to have a place.

Closely connected with the infallibility and authority of holy scripture, and belonging to the basis on which we must proceed in the discussion of the creation record, is the truth that scripture is perspicuous. It is not obscure or dark, but clear—so clear that any child of God can understand it. One need not be a theologian, an exegete, a scientist, or some other well-educated expert to understand the scriptures. Any child of God can apprehend the truth revealed in them. This is fundamental. If scripture is not perspicuous, it is for the most part a closed book. The perspicuity or clarity of scripture belongs to our Reformation heritage, and it forms an important part of the basis on which to proceed.

The Issue: Creation versus Evolution

The issue concerning the creation record is creation versus evolution.

What is creation? Creation is the act of the almighty will of God whereby through his word and by his Spirit he gave to the entire universe, and to all the individual creatures of that universe, (things as they eternally exist in God's eternal counsel) existence in distinction from himself and his own being.

The theory of evolution is diametrically opposed to the truth of creation.

The theory of evolution maintains that the world began somehow of itself. The theory holds that from an early but unexplained and obscure beginning, the universe gradually evolved and developed. This development allegedly began first in the inorganic, nonliving, creature. It took definite shape, form, and place in the whole of the universe through evolution. It evolved and developed from the less refined and less definite to the more refined and the more definite. Then somehow in that evolving universe a principle of life came into being, and all the forms of the organic, living creature developed out of one cell, the one seed of life. Things developed from lower to higher forms, from simple to complex forms. Man is a product of such development. Evolutionism holds that all things developed over hundreds of millions and even billions of years, until the world and the human race as we now know it came into existence.

Evolutionism includes much more than this. It is concerned not only with the origin of all things, but it is also an entire philosophy of the world and of history. This far-reaching philosophy of the world and of history is inseparably connected with evolutionism's theory of the origin of all things, but these other aspects, though important, are not part of the present discussion.

In What Sense
Is Evolutionism the Issue?

You probably say, "But in the above sense evolutionism cannot be an issue and a question for the child of God." I agree. We are not surprised that unbelief, the outstanding sin of the world, invents its own theory of the beginning of the world, a beginning without God. Unbelief wants to get God out of the world, and in order to get God out of the world, it aims to get God out of the beginning. If he is out of the beginning, he is out of this world entirely. God is not in all the thoughts of the unbeliever, even the religious unbeliever.

From that viewpoint it is below the dignity of faith, the dignity of the Christian, to enter into any scientific debate whatsoever with the evolutionist. Why try to meet him on his own ground without the Bible? Why try to gainsay by human logic and ingenuity such a monstrosity of sin as the theory of evolution? The Christian says rather, "In the beginning *God*" The Christian says rather, "Give me God, and I can explain the world. Take my God away, and I must sit down in despair." For, "through faith we understand that the worlds were framed by the word of God, so that things which are seen were not made of things which do appear" (Heb. 11:3). The evolutionist is like the fool who desires to employ his human keenness to show me that I had no father and that I was not born. All one can do with such attempts is to turn away in complete disgust.

In its blunt, direct form, evolutionism cannot be and is not an issue for the Christian and the church.

However, the theory of evolution has been developed and refined so that it has become more insidious in the form called theistic evolutionism, or in more palatable terminology, progressive creationism. Although progressive creationism is a refinement in terminology, it is the same as theistic evolutionism.

The theory of theistic evolution as an explanation of the origin of the world seeks to maintain all the tenets of evolutionism, but attempts to insert God into the process of evolution as an intelligent and controlling power. Theistic evolutionism maintains that God created the principle of all things, and then that divinely created principle of all things evolved or developed along the lines in which unbelieving evolutionism presents it as evolving. The theory of theistic evolution maintains that God never works in this universe except through ordinary ways, by second causes, or according to what are called natural laws. Even creation is by law. God uses the physical laws of the universe to produce specifically new things. New species or kinds are produced in the vegetable and in the animal world. Man himself is produced according to those same physical laws and out of the same originally created principle of life. All things have developed out of original matter or from an original life-cell according to divine design and purpose, and as a result of divine operation through second causes and natural laws.

One can say many things about theistic evolutionism, for it is really an entire philosophy, a world and life view. If you begin with evolutionism of any kind, you must adopt the whole theory, and you must end where evolutionism ends. Historically the adoption of evolutionistic theories concerning the origin of things has led exactly to that consequence. The same holds for the adoption of theistic evolution. For example, in the area of eschatology it has led to postmillennial conceptions.

Through the adoption of theistic evolution the element of the miraculous is also eliminated. It is first eliminated from the origin of the universe. Because the theory proceeds on the basis that God never works in this universe except through ordinary ways and according to natural laws, inevitably the wonder is eliminated everywhere. This also is history. When the leaven of this theory has worked through, the result has been that the wonder of grace is completely eliminated and denied. For all the miracles some naturalistic explanation is found, and the historical reality of such wonders as the incarnation and the resurrection of our Lord Jesus Christ is also denied.

Theistic evolutionism is an attempted compromise. It is an attempted synthesis of worldly theory and philosophy and of scriptural truth. It is an attempted mixture of the lie and the truth.

Such compromise never works. The truth and the lie simply cannot be mixed. If such a mixture is attempted, the result is inevitably that the truth is denied. Theistic evolutionism—contrary to its claims to be creationism and to be theistic—does not really believe the creation record. At the basis of the position of theistic evolutionism is a fundamentally wrong method and approach. Theistic evolutionism does not operate from the principle of the antithesis between the truth and the lie, of faith and unbelief, but from the principle of synthesis. This principle of synthesis is the principle of world conformity. The attempt is made to synthesize creationism and evolutionism, theism and atheistic philosophy, biblical faith and worldly science, scripture and the rationalistic, unbelieving theories and hypotheses of worldly science. Such a mixture never works because you cannot mix opposites. The result of an attempted mixture is always a denial of the truth.

This is also the result practically. Inquire as to what receives the emphasis in theistic evolutionism. Is it theism that is emphasized? Not at all; the theism is never emphasized until evolutionism comes under attack. The theory tries to allow room for the theory of evolution and at the same time to allow room for the evolutionist to say, "I believe in God too." The same is true of the supposedly more palatable expression progressive creationism. In practice it puts all the emphasis on progressive and leaves creationism out of the picture. This is done in order to go along as much as possible with worldly evolutionary theory. When criticism of this progressivism arises, the progressive creationist thinks he can respond to that criticism by saying, "But I believe in creation too, except that my idea of creation is that it was progressive." From a practical viewpoint theism and creationism come crippling behind the evolutionism and the progressivism of these theories.

By that attempted mixture, the issue of creation versus evolution as an explanation of the origin of the world has found its way into the church. This has become an issue not only in the church at large, but also in the Reformed community of churches, both in the Netherlands and in the United States. In its blunt and direct form the theory of evolution cannot be an issue for a church that claims to adhere to scripture. But under the form of theistic evolutionism and progressive creationism the cargo of the evolutionary theory has been smuggled into the church, and thus creation doctrine versus evolutionism has become an issue in the church. This brand of evolutionism has made no small degree of progress even in Reformed circles. Books and articles are written that uphold and promote the theory. It is taught in the schools. Especially in certain educated and scientific circles what is referred to as the traditional creationist view has come under open attack as an impossible, preposterous, and grossly old-fashioned theory.

The Literal or Nonliteral Issue

In connection with that introduction into the church of what is claimed to be a Christian and biblical brand of evolutionism, the literal or nonliteral character of the creation record has become an issue confronting the church today.

How does this become the issue?

First, progressive creationism comes face-to-face with the creation record. Evolutionism is not troubled by this. Simple, blunt evolutionism has nothing to do with creationism. It denies all creation. It is a theory that places itself over against all creation faith. But the compromise theory necessarily confronts the creation record of scripture. It is a theory that arises in the church, not in the world. It is a theory that claims to be consistent with belief in God, the creator. It is a theory that claims to be just a modification of biblical creation and to be consistent with belief in the doctrine of creation. Hence it is a theory that must reckon with holy scripture and that somehow must take into account what the Bible says about creation.

Second, the theory of theistic evolution comes face-to-face with the time element in Genesis I. There are many other connected difficulties that the theory faces in the biblical record when it attempts to reconcile this theory with the statements of scripture concerning creation, but the most crucial problem is time. Evolution requires time. It needs large quantities of time. It needs millions upon millions and hundreds of millions and even billions of years. This is a well-known characteristic of evolutionism, and it is also a chief characteristic of theistic evolutionism and progressive creationism. The processes of evolution really cannot be explained; all the riddles of evolution are hidden in the dim reaches of those billions of years. In this connection scientists have developed many alleged evidences of such long periods of time in the history of the universe. When theistic evolutionism, with its requirement of billions of years, comes face-to-face with the scriptural record of creation in Genesis I, it faces the necessity of making room in the presentation of Genesis I for those long periods of time. And what is the conclusion? Does the theistic evolutionist arrive at the conclusion that Genesis I simply does not allow room for billions of years, and that therefore he must drop his theory of evolutionism? Not at all. On the contrary, he interprets Genesis I to fit his theory.

Third, this gives rise to the question of the historicity of the record of creation in Genesis. Is the creation record the record of historical facts, the record of historical events? Did the things recorded in Genesis I actually take place as they are recorded? That question is unavoidable because with historicity stands or falls the reality, the factualness of the creative work. Either Genesis is a revelation of real, historical, factual events, and God's work of creation actually took place, or Genesis is not the record of real, historical, factual events, and then the creation and the act of creation are not facts.

To this unavoidable question concerning the historicity of the creation record the theistic evolutionist must try to give an affirmative answer. As a theist the theistic evolutionist feels bound to do so; and as a creationist, the progressive creationist feels compelled to answer affirmatively. After all, it is an article of the Christian faith: "I believe in God the Father, Almighty, Maker of heaven and earth." Hence creationists must and do attempt to maintain somehow that the creation record is a historic fact, but they do so on their own terms. In answer to the question concerning historicity, they say, "Yes, provided we interpret Genesis 1 and 2 (and Genesis 3 to an extent) correctly." By "correctly" they mean the way they want to interpret it. They must find ways and means of maintaining that the creation record is not ordinary history, not even ordinary sacred history, but history that is recorded in some unusual, strange way. They must keep the language of Genesis, but pour into it a content that harmonizes with their evolutionistic and progressivist theories.

In this way various theories of interpretation have arisen and are maintained today in order to accommodate that alleged scientific evidence and the theory of theistic evolution, which requires millions and billions of years.

For this reason it is impossible to be satisfied only with the question, is the creation record historical? That allows room for evasion of the issue. You must specify. You must pinpoint the issue. You must find out what the theistic evolutionists mean by *historical*. Therefore you must ask, is the creation record literally historical? Is it to be interpreted literally or nonliterally?

An Exegetical Question

This is a matter of scripture, the infallible word of God, and as surely as it concerns scripture, so surely it involves exegesis.

Absolutely nothing outside of scripture—no science, no scientific theory, no rationalism, no self-made doubts and questions, no theological opinions—may enter into the answer to this question. It is strictly an exegetical question, a question of scripture and scripture's meaning, a question of the authority of scripture. Exegesis is concerned with the meaning of the word of God. Exegesis inquires into the meaning of the word of God. It presupposes that the word of God is understandable, that it is clear and perspicuous, and that therefore the truth of the word of God can be readily ascertained. Ultimately exegesis bows before the divine authority of the word of God. The decisive question is not what this or that theologian thinks. In coming to a conclusion on this issue it is of absolutely no benefit to engage in name dropping. No matter how much respect we may have for certain church fathers, and no matter how much we may respect their learning and their contributions to the development of doctrine, it is not a question of whether or not some of the early church fathers maintained the period theory or the framework theory. Apparently some did so. It is not a question of whether Abraham Kuyper or Herman Bavinck allowed room for leaving the days of creation longer than normal days, nor is it a question of what Herman Hoeksema taught or of what Homer Hoeksema thinks about this matter. Neither is it a question of what this or that church thinks about this issue or has expressed officially about it. Ultimately this is not even a question of what this or that confession says. The confessions also are subject solely to the authority of scripture, and they have authority only insofar as they express the truth of holy scripture. In other words, the Bible is the only court of appeal in this discussion.

This is the cardinal principle of the Reformed faith. It is the plain teaching of the Belgic Confession in article 7. That article speaks of the sufficiency of scripture as the only rule of faith. It states the following: "Neither may we compare any writings of men, though ever so holy, with those divine Scriptures; nor ought we to compare custom, or the great multitude, or antiquity, or succession of times or persons, or councils, decrees, or statutes, with the truth of God, for the truth is above all: for all men are of themselves liars, and more vain than vanity itself."[1] Nothing else is to be placed in equal authority next to the scriptures.

Exegesis is an exact science. There is much talk about science, scientific evidence, and the exactness and fool-proofness of science in connection with this subject of origins. The position is sometimes taken that one must be a fool to quarrel with science's alleged discoveries and evidences, and that to disagree with what the scientists say

---

[1] Belgic Confession 7, in Schaff, *Creeds of Christendom*, 3:388.

about the age of the world is to fly in the face of facts and incontrovertible evidence. In conflict with that attitude, the exegesis of holy scripture is also a science. It is the practical science of the interpretation of scripture. If there was ever a science that is exact and that requires exactitude, it is the science of exegesis. Exegesis takes place according to certain definite rules. The most fundamental of those rules is that scripture itself must interpret scripture. That is a simple but fundamental rule. Scripture must speak for itself. Our interpretations must indeed be interpretations. They must not stand in the way of the speech of scripture. An interpretation of scripture must be the one, necessary interpretation demanded by scripture itself.

Moreover, exegesis must be unbiased. Science likes to speak of being unbiased and unprepossessed as a fundamental tenet of the scientific method. We may accept that in the good sense, and we do accept that also with application to exegesis. The exegete must approach scripture without any prepossession, except the prepossession or the bias of faith. He must not attempt to give his own opinion about the word of God, but he must let the word of God speak. The bias of faith means that he is prepared to listen and to bow unconditionally before the authority of scripture.

The Nonliteral and Literal Views

Some nonliteral interpretations of scripture immediately can be ruled out. They are not maintained in any orthodox church. They are not only nonliteral, but they are altogether nonbiblical and unbelieving. They are farfetched in relation to the biblical record. They are distant too as far as maintaining any truth of creation is concerned, and the Bible-believing child of God must spontaneously react against these theories. Among these nonliteral theories is the mythical theory, which holds that Genesis is Israel's myth concerning the origin of things. Many ancient nations had such myths, and Israel also had such a myth, possibly borrowed from one or more of the other nations. That is unbelief. It involves higher criticism. It denies the divine inspiration and infallibility of the Genesis record, and faith cannot even consider such a theory. In the same category are the allegorical and poetical theories. They deny not only the literal character of the Genesis record, but they also deny the historicity of creation altogether. These theories are not very much in vogue today. We need not concern ourselves with them because they are too obviously contrary to the entire presentation of Genesis: they do not even have a semblance of being interpretations, but are superimposed on the text. There is not the slightest hint in Genesis, nor anywhere in scripture, that Genesis I is allegory or poetry. I would also include in this group the saga theory of Karl Barth. We do not need to describe this theory in detail or be troubled by it, because Barth denied the infallibility of scripture. On the basis of that denial there is no common ground for discussion.

However, there are several more proximate and more current theories. Three of them are known as the concordistic theories.

The first of these is the restitution theory, which teaches that Genesis I:I records the creation of a first world, but following that first creation there was a series of mighty catastrophes that destroyed it and left it "without form and void," and that out of this desolation the present universe was formed by a second creative act. This theory is not popular now, at least insofar as it presents this world as a restitution of a previous world. Its advantage is supposedly that it leaves an indefinite time gap between verse 1 and verse 3 of Genesis 1, and thus leaves room for a long period of time. However, it also has a notable disadvantage for the theistic evolutionist in that it does not leave enough room for his theory and for the remainder of creation week. The progressivist or evolutionist needs such room for his theory not only on or before the first day, but also throughout creation week.

The most popular and widely accepted of these concordistic theories is the period theory, which interprets the term "day" in Genesis 1 as a period of hundreds of millions of years. Each of the six successive days of creation week was such a long period of time. Thus as far as the crucial time element is concerned, this theory makes room for the possibility of theistic evolution or progressive creation. All things came into being not in six twenty-four hour days (which is impossible, according to this theory), but over the course of billions of years.

A third theory does not tamper with the days of creation week, but inserts between those days a period of many millions of years. This is known as the inter-period theory, which also allows the necessary time for a process of evolution. However, this theory is not very commonly held today.

Finally, as far as the proximate nonliteral interpretations are concerned, there is the framework theory. The theory itself is not new, but recently it has become more popular among those who do not hold to the literal creation interpretation. To be fair, I want to let an advocate of this theory tell us what he means by it. The following is quoted from N. H. Ridderbos:

> By the framework-hypothesis I mean the following. In Genesis I the inspired author offers us a story of creation. It is not his intent, however, to present an exact report of what happened at creation. By speaking of the eightfold work of God he impresses the reader with the fact that all that exists has been created by God. The eightfold work he places in a frame-work; he distributes it over six days, to which he adds a seventh day as the day of rest. In this manner he gives expression

to the fact that the work of creation is complete; also that at the conclusion of His work God can rest, take delight in the result; and also (cf. pp. 40–42) that in celebrating the Sabbath man must be God's imitator. The manner in which the works of creation have been distributed over six days is not arbitrary (see pp. 32–35).[2]

The framework hypothesis seems to succeed in maintaining that Genesis is inspired. It speaks of the inspired author. It seems also to maintain that creation is historical; it actually took place. But note that Genesis I is called "a story of creation," and Ridderbos claims that it is not the inspired author's intent "to present an exact report of what happened at creation." Further, the framework hypothesis seems to preserve the idea of the six days of creation week. However, those six days are only a literary framework into which the inspired author placed God's work of creation. They are not the framework in

---

2 N. H. Ridderbos, *Is There a Conflict between Genesis 1 and Natural Science?* (Grand Rapids, MI: William B. Eerdmans Publishing Company, 1957), 45

which the act of creation actually took place, but the literary framework in which the report of creation has been placed by the author of Genesis. This framework of six days is not a reported historical event, but something that has been imposed upon the divine work of creation. The days are not real. Genesis I says nothing about the actual time and order of creation. It tells us nothing whatsoever about how long it took to create, or when God created, or whether God actually created in six days. This theory leaves the question of the exact historical event of creation, the time of creation, and the duration of the creation work wide open for the theory of theistic evolution. With some the framework hypothesis has become more popular than the period theory. The framework hypothesis solves all of the troublesome problems of theistic evolutionism.

There are also a number of more literal theories. One is that the days of creation week were real days, but not ordinary, twenty-four hour days. This is the view of G. C. Aalders (1880–1960), a liberal theologian in Kampen, the Netherlands. Concerning these real days, which were not ordinary days, he writes, "They need not have lasted longer than our days, they may have been much shorter;

they may by our chronometric standards have lasted only a few seconds." I cannot understand the necessity for such a presentation. What are real days that are not ordinary days? Our only point of comparison for the conception of a real day is the day we know, that is, a twenty-four hour day. When scripture speaks of days and in every way refers to them in terms of the only days that we know, we have no recourse but to understand those days as ordinary days. This is entirely apart from the question whether those days were not ordinary, but extraordinary from the viewpoint of their events.

Other exegetes hold to the view that creation took place in six ordinary days, but they do not consider the days to be a crucial issue of interpretation, and they do not regard as binding that the days were indeed six ordinary days of twenty-four hours.

In distinction from all of the above theories is the literal interpretation of the Genesis record (sometimes called the realistic view), namely, that God created the universe on six consecutive days, limited by morning and evening, that is, six real, ordinary days like our days of twenty-four hours.

Evaluation

How must we evaluate and judge these various theories?

I do not intend to criticize each theory in detail and to examine the various arguments advanced in support of each, nor do I intend to examine and to answer every objection that is raised against the literal interpretation. This is not necessary. I want instead to consider something more fundamental.

Consider with me these theories with Genesis 1 in hand. Some of these theories are elaborately devised. Some of them have what are claimed to be scriptural arguments behind them. But let us put them to the test of scripture without anything additional—the test of scripture approached unprepossessed, except for faith—the test of scripture as any ordinary child of God can read the scriptures and understand them.

Take, for example, the period theory. Genesis 1 speaks of six successive days in which God created. It speaks of days that are delineated by evening and morning. It speaks already with respect to the first day of a distinction between the light and the darkness, between day and night. Can those days by any stretch of exegesis be changed into periods of hundreds of millions of years? Is that actually a matter of interpretation? Can an appeal properly be made to the idea that this is all a matter of how one interprets Genesis I?

To ask such a question is to answer it.

By definition such an interpretation is impossible. A day delineated by morning and evening and consisting of day and night simply is not a period of millions of years. A year is already a large number of days, and a period of millions of years certainly cannot correctly be described as such an ordinary day. That is plainly the case by definition.

You can test that theory and the above objection by paraphrasing the text in Genesis in terms of periods. Let us read Genesis I as though it spoke of periods of hundreds of millions of years. It does not even begin to make sense. What becomes of a verse like Genesis I:5 when you do that? This: "And God called the light day, and the darkness he called night. And the evening and the morning were the first two hundred million years." Or again, in Genesis I:8: "And the evening and the morning were the second two hundred million years." Or try this with the fourth commandment, which makes clear reference to the creation ordinance: "Six days shalt thou labor and do all thy work: but the seventh day is the sabbath of the LORD thy God...For in six periods of two hundred million years the LORD made heaven and earth, the sea, and all that in them is, and rested the seventh period of two hundred million years: wherefore the LORD blessed the sabbath period of two hundred million years, and hallowed it." Obviously, this interpretation is absurd. It is sheer nonsense. It cannot legitimately be called an interpretation. Remember that Genesis 1 is perspicuous scripture. Any child of God is able to read it and to understand it. What becomes of perspicuous scripture when it must be understood in this fashion?

Other claims are made in connection with the period theory. The attempt is made to give it some scriptural and exegetical foundation, but these attempts fail, one and all. For example, appeal is made to 2 Peter 3:8: "But, beloved, be not ignorant of this one thing, that one day is with the Lord as a thousand years, and a thousand years as one day." Apart from any other considerations and apart from the fact that the text is obviously speaking basically of God's eternity and of the fact that God does not view time as we view it, the last part of this text is conveniently overlooked: "and a thousand years as one day." But above all, 2 Peter does not *identify* one day and a thousand years, but *compares* the two with respect to God: "One day is with the Lord *as* a thousand years, and a thousand years *as* one day."

Appeal is also made to the Sabbath of the seventh day. The claim is made that when scripture tells us that God rested on the seventh day, that day cannot possibly be taken as a twenty-four hour day, because the Sabbath never ends for God: he does not rest for twenty-four hours, but eternally. That argument is exegetically specious, for the Sabbath of the seventh day can only be the *revelation* of God's eternal rest into which man enters in time. But if you accept the proposed exegesis of the period theoreticians for a moment, and if you apply their argument, you soon discover that it proves far too much. The result is not periods of a few hundred million years, but *unending periods*. If the Sabbath of the seventh day is unending, then all the first six long periods were unending. This is the only possible conclusion on the basis of the sound rule of exegesis that the same term in the same connection means

69

the same thing unless there are clear reasons in the text and context that it should not mean the same thing.

The same objection can be applied to the framework theory as to the period theory. It claims to have some arguments in its favor. But if you put away your theistic evolutionary eyeglasses and your prepossessions, put out of your mind for the moment so-called scientific evidences, and simply read and let scripture speak, then the framework hypothesis does not fit the text of Genesis. It is preposterous! You cannot find a hint of it in the text. From an exegetical viewpoint, when you read the record of Genesis I, the framework hypothesis leaves the impression of being nothing less than a cunningly devised fable.

What an altogether strange impression the infallible and perspicuous word of God in Genesis I must make on the unsuspecting reader if the framework hypothesis is true! How altogether impossible it becomes to read any historical account and to grasp its meaning and message if this is the way that scripture must be read! One would always need an expert theologian and exegete near at hand if the scriptures were to be read in this fashion. Genesis I leaves no other impression than that of an exact report of the wonderful work of creation day by day. But according to the framework hypothesis, we must always read Genesis as a creation story, not as an exact report. Scripture does not tell us what God actually did. You can distill out of it the fact that somehow all that exists has been created by God. You can extract from it that the work of God was eightfold. You can conclude from it that the work of creation is complete, that at the conclusion of it God can rest and take delight in the result, and that in celebrating the Sabbath man must be God's imitator. But that is all. When all is said and done, you know nothing as to what actually took place. Moreover, when Genesis speaks of six days and leaves no impression on any reader other than that they were six days, you must remember that there were not really six days, but that the scheme of six days plus one day is only an artificial scheme, a literary framework, into which the very vague and inexactly reported work of creation is fitted.

How strange! How impossible it becomes to read and understand scripture in this way!

The attempt is made to find scriptural support for the possibility of the framework interpretation. Something akin to such a framework is supposed to be found in "the book of the generation of Jesus Christ" in Matthew I. There scripture presents an artificial or schematic arrangement of the generations of Jesus Christ, not an exact chronological and genealogical line. Some generations are skipped. You find there three times a set of fourteen, or two times seven generations. Matthew I is far from a literary framework. It is correct that certain generations are skipped, and that due to these omissions there is no exact chronological and genealogical line in Matthew I. But does that make it a framework? By no means, for the overall presentation is that of a progressive genealogy from Abraham to Christ, which is far different from the vague literary framework postulated for Genesis I. Further, scripture suggests that in Matthew I there is a schematic arrangement of the generations of Jesus Christ. In verse 17 of that chapter we read: "So all the generations from Abraham to David are fourteen generations; and from David until the carrying away into Babylon are fourteen generations; and from the carrying away into Babylon unto Christ are fourteen generations." Besides, we have the evidence of scripture itself in the Old Testament that there are generations that have been omitted from the series in Matthew. Hence Matthew I is not an instance of scripture's fraudulently foisting an inexact story on an unsuspecting reader, as is the case with the framework hypothesis of Genesis I. Nor is it difficult at all to interpret Matthew I in complete harmony with the fundamental rule of exegesis that scripture must interpret scripture, a rule that is violated by the framework hypothesis as imposed on Genesis I without any ground, without any occasion being offered by scripture itself, and without any clear, incontrovertible scriptural warrant.

Negatively, this is the significance of the principle that we must proceed exegetically with respect to Genesis I. One must not *impose* alleged interpretations upon scripture. One must not suggest abstractly possible explanations. One must show by incontrovertible evidence from the text, from the immediate context, and from the broader context of the whole of scripture, that a given explanation is the only possible meaning of the text, which is on a scriptural basis absolutely necessary. Moreover, in order to make way for such a nonliteral interpretation, one must first show with incontrovertible evidence from scripture itself—not from science or from claimed scientific data—that the literal interpretation is absolutely impossible, and that therefore scripture demands some other kind of interpretation.

That is sound exegetical practice. That is responsible exegesis.

The Proper Scriptural Interpretation

On the above basis, the literal interpretation of creation stands.

God created.

He did not providentially control and cause all things to develop in that creation work. He did not operate through second causes and according to natural laws, as he is sometimes presented as doing in his work of providence. The work of creation and the work of providence, both divine works, are not to be confused. In creation God does not uphold and govern all things according to so-called natural laws—more correctly, creation ordinances—but he laid down those creation ordinances in the beginning.

He spoke, and it was done; he commanded, and it stood fast. By the word of the Lord were the heavens made, and all the host of them by the breath of his mouth. God spoke his word of power. That was real speech. It was divine speech; but it was real, literal speech of God, producing what it uttered: "Let there be light...let there be a firmament...let the dry land appear...let the earth bring forth grass, the herb yielding seed, and the fruit tree... let there be luminaries in the firmament of the heaven... let the waters bring forth abundantly...let the earth bring forth the living creature after his kind...let us make man in our image." By that almighty speech of God everything was produced. Moreover, all the creative works of God took place in six ordinary days, but not because God needed twenty-four hours to create one kind of creature. He did not, no more than he needs millions of years. But God created in six ordinary days simply because the Bible says so. That is all, and that is enough for faith. I ask you to bow with me before scripture. With that creation God also created time, and he created in the entire universe the week, the six plus the one, the labor plus the Sabbath. Thus all creation is the direct product of his sovereign will.

Such is the presentation of scripture. Not a hint of anything different is ever found in scripture. That can only come from outside of scripture. This is not to say that there are no exegetical difficulties or problems with respect to the details of the work of creation. There are some. Nor does the maintenance of the literal creation interpretation imply that we can comprehend or fathom the wonderful work of God. God is incomprehensible in all his works. The creature can fathom only a speech that calls things that are. He cannot comprehend the speech of God whereby he calls the things that are not and whereby things that are made were not formed from things which do appear (Rom. 4:17; Heb. 11:3). This in no wise detracts from the reality and the factualness of the wonderwork of God, and this in no wise warrants any kind of naturalistic and evolutionistic presentation. All scripture speaks one language with respect to creation and the creative act, turn where you will. Genesis, Hebrews 11, John 1, Colossians 1, and Psalm 33 all speak the same language.

The result of that creative work of the Almighty was that the whole creation, God's handiwork, the product of his word, was very good as it stood in its pristine perfection under its first head and king, Adam. It was all designed to serve man, in order that man, reading God's word in all the works of his Creator, could tell God's wonderful works and serve his God.

Because all this is intimately connected with the gospel, from the historical point of that "very good" at the conclusion of creation, the line is not the evolutionistic line onward and upward, from good to better to best. The line is downward. It is the line of the fall into sin and death and the curse. Why? Because God with his first creation had in view his better purpose for his people in Christ Jesus. The first world was designed with a view to the second world, the heavenly creation, where all things will be united in Christ Jesus our Lord. The first world was designed to serve as the stage for the beautiful drama of sin and grace, the drama of redemption. It was to serve as the stage for the perfect realization of God's everlasting covenant of grace in Christ Jesus. Thus, created by God's hand and providentially controlled by his hand, the world moves from the beginning (*bereshith*) of Genesis I, to the end (*telos*) of all things, the final consummation in the day of our Lord Jesus Christ. It *can* do so because it is God's world. It *will* do so because it is God's world.

Then he who created all things in the beginning will make all things new in the way of the final catastrophe and the final wonder of grace. Then all the scoffers, who maintain that things continue as they were in the beginning, will be put to naught, and God's people will sing the praises of their Creator forever.

In that sense, the world is my Father's world—the world of "the eternal Father of our Lord Jesus Christ, who of nothing made heaven and earth, with all that in them is, who likewise upholds and governs the same by his eternal counsel and providence," and who "is for the sake of Christ his Son my God and my Father."[3]

This is the simple and perspicuous truth that we confess when we say, "I believe in God the Father, Almighty, Maker of heaven and earth."[4] This is the language, unencumbered by the compromising weight of any evolutionism or progressivism, that we find in the Belgic Confession: "We believe that the Father, by the Word—

---

3 Heidelberg Catechism A 27, in Schaff, *Creeds of Christendom*, 3:315

4 Apostles' Creed, in *The Confessions and the Church Order of the Protestant Reformed Churches* (Grandville, MI: Protestant Reformed Churches in America, 2005), 9.

that is, by his Son—created of nothing the heaven, the earth, and all creatures, as it seemed good unto him, giving unto every creature its being, shape, form, and several offices to serve its Creator."[5] This is the speech of faith.

But what about all the scientific evidences? What about the results of natural science? Even if all those evidences cannot be explained, scripture stands, and the believer must without compromise stand strictly on its basis. However, I believe that the literal Genesis record and true science are entirely compatible. Let the church and the believer stand fast on this only foundation of scripture!

---

5 Belgic Confession 12, in Schaff, *Creeds of Christendom*, 3:395

Chapter 3

GENESIS AND SCIENCE

I call attention first to the formulation of the subject of this chapter: Genesis and science. The material of this chapter goes beyond the more limited subject of creation and science. The maintenance of the creation doctrine in connection with some of the scientific data and evidences that have been collected and that are frequently used to deny the truth of creation is involved in this discussion. In a way this is even our chief interest. However, a proper discussion of this subject must go beyond the creation record. To an increasing extent in current discussions, both on the part of those who deny the truth of creation and on the part of those who maintain it, the entire first eleven chapters of the book of Genesis have become involved. As will become evident, a Christian view of science in relation to the truth of creation must take into account much more of scripture, and particularly of Genesis, than the creation record of Genesis 1 and 2. Ultimately the whole principle of scripture itself, and the whole content of scripture become involved in this discussion. But I will concentrate especially on Genesis in relation to science.

Second, I emphasize that this chapter does not concern Genesis versus science or science versus Genesis. That would imply that there is a conflict between the two, and I do not believe that there is such a conflict. Genesis and science are quite compatible. As soon as you pervert science into a religion or a set of beliefs that is opposed to Genesis, you no longer have science, but *scientism*. But scripture and science, properly conceived, are compatible. Otherwise a Christian could not be a scientist. Hence the discussion in this chapter centers on Genesis and science. We are interested in the relation between Genesis and science and between Genesis and some of the data science has compiled and that are pertinent to this subject. We are also interested in Genesis in relation to some of the allegedly scientific conclusions that have been reached and that are maintained in connection with what Genesis teaches concerning creation.

The subject of this chapter naturally arises out of the position taken in the previous chapter, in which I stated, strictly on the basis of scripture, that the doctrine of creation must be literally maintained, and that on the basis of clear and simple exegesis of the word of God, it must be maintained that creation took place in six real, ordinary, twenty-four hour days. I suggested that this position raises questions concerning all the alleged scientific data and claimed scientific evidence that seem to contradict the literal creation doctrine. To those questions this chapter is devoted.

Before entering into the discussion of this subject, I make a few observations as to my approach.

First, as I maintained in the previous chapter, I insist that the literal creation doctrine does not depend on science or on scientific evidences, nor does it depend on one's ability or inability to explain any alleged scientific evidences to the contrary. This point I deem very important, as I hope will become increasingly clear. This is the strength of the Christian's position. His belief in the literal creation doctrine depends on the Bible, and on the Bible alone. Even if I could not explain the data produced by science at all, and even if no suggestion of an explanation could be made, I would nevertheless maintain the literal creation doctrine solely on the basis of scripture. This is simply a matter of the authority and sufficiency of scripture.

That this constitutes the strength of the Christian's position has often been forgotten, and is often forgotten today. People of God have allowed themselves to be swayed by influences other than the authoritative influence of holy scripture. That is wrong. It is a violation of the principle of the authority of scripture. There are scientists today, also Christian scientists, who sneer at that. They call it fundamentalism, and they claim that it is three hundred years behind the times. That makes no difference to me, because this sneering constitutes neither a Christian attitude nor a sound argument.

Second, although we are dealing in this chapter with science, my approach is not that of a scientist. I am not a scientist. I would not even dare to call myself an amateur scientist, and I certainly do not write these lines as a scientist.

However, I do not mention this as an apology or an excuse, nor do I mention it because I have no respect for scientific disciplines and research. The contrary is true. I believe that science is proper and that scientific research is beneficial and necessary. Moreover, I believe that the area of science is a proper one for the Christian's labors. I am not opposing science.

But I mention this because it affects my approach to this subject. I believe also that a good scientist can meet and destroy many of the arguments of an evolutionistic scientist on a scientific basis and can show those arguments to be grossly unscientific. I will make a few passing references to such attempts, but my emphasis will not be on that aspect of our subject, nor will my fundamental approach be scientific. There is a deeper reason that that will not be my approach: the heart of a sound defense of the faith, the heart of what is called in theology a sound apologetics, is biblical, not rationalistic. On that biblical basis I will approach the subject of this chapter. The question that confronts us with respect to every aspect of life, science included, is, what does the word of God say?

What Is Science?

In discussing the relation between Genesis and science we must have a clear understanding of these terms. What is Genesis? And what is science?

To summarize the previous two chapters, Genesis is the infallible record of the revelation of God in Christ concerning the beginning of all things. Genesis is perspicuous or clear, and Genesis is literal sacred history that teaches the literal creation doctrine expounded in the previous chapter.

What is science?

The term *science* comes from the Latin word *scientia*, which means "knowledge." True science is knowledge, and as a discipline, science aims at discovering knowledge. The definition furnished by the *Oxford Dictionary* will serve our purpose. Science is "a branch of study that is concerned either with a connected body of demonstrated truths or with observed facts systematically classified and more or less colligated by being brought under general laws, and that includes trustworthy methods for the discovery of new truths within its own domain."

Science is concerned with facts and laws that have been demonstrated. This is the limitation of all true science. Any alleged science or scientific conclusion that goes beyond this limitation of demonstrated or demonstrable facts and laws has no right to the name science. Further, the scientific method involves experimentation and experimental reproducibility. Moreover, it is in the nature of science that it is strictly limited to the measurement and study of present phenomena and processes. Those things that can be or have been observed and studied in the present, or such data as have been recorded by men in the past are the proper objects of scientific study, investigation, and knowledge.

At this point it is necessary to point out that science is not inference, speculation, or speculative theory. Science is bound to observed facts and demonstrated truths, and it is limited to the present and the historic past. This is characteristic of science from a formal viewpoint— and science is a formal discipline. It is precisely at this juncture that a formal and scientific problem arises in connection with the subject of this chapter and in connection with evolutionistic theory. This is frequently forgotten. The attitude is assumed that evolutionism is highly scientific and that belief in a literal six-day creation is extremely unscientific. The two are portrayed as opposing each other, as though the one who believes in creation blindly flies in the face of science. Also those who attempt to compromise between creation and evolution like to present matters as though belief in strict, biblical creation is scientifically absurd. However, much of what is claimed to be science and scientific conclusion is not science, but inference and speculative conclusion that has supposedly been made on the basis of and in the name of science. This is a good distinction to keep in mind when approaching this entire discussion from a strictly formal, scientific viewpoint.

Although we can accept the above formal definition of science, this definition is barren. For a correct understanding of our subject it is necessary to probe a bit deeper into the nature of science in relation to Genesis.

From the deeper, spiritual viewpoint we must remember that true knowledge is always knowledge of God. "The knowledge of the holy is understanding," Proverbs 9:10 says, and that also holds true for science. True science is ultimately concerned with the knowledge of God. It must stand in the service of the knowledge of God, and it must end in the knowledge of God. If it fails to do so, it is not true science. For that reason, even though science is a formal discipline and as far as its formal methods are concerned, it is much the same for believer and unbeliever, we must always keep in mind that science is more than a formal discipline. It includes interpretation. It includes not only the formal interpretation of certain data, but also the spiritual interpretation of it and the application of all the scientific data and conclusions with respect to the knowledge of God. Thus a learned scientist may be a gross fool and an ignoramus if with all his scientific learning he does not end in the knowledge of God and is not subject to the knowledge of God as revealed in the scriptures. In that case he is not a true scientist, but the antithesis of a scientist. The fact that science is essentially knowledge of God from the outset rules out evolutionistic science, for the science of the evolutionist exactly denies God. His science is not true knowledge because it is not knowledge of God. It is the opposite of knowledge, and the spiritual opposite of knowledge is the ignorance of the lie. At this point the Christian parts ways with the evolutionist.

The Scientist and Revelation

From a biblical and spiritual viewpoint another question is must be asked. What is the relation between Genesis with its creation record and science with its scientific investigation and data?

This question involves the truth that God's revelation is twofold. There is his revelation in holy scripture and his revelation in all the works of his hands. However, God's revelation is one. There are not two different, unconnected revelations of God, but one twofold revelation. To its second aspect, sometimes mistakenly called general revelation, belongs the entire universe and all the history of that universe—God's works in creation and in providence.

With the book of God in nature, in creation, and

in the works of his hands every scientist works. He cannot avoid that. No matter what part of God's creation he labors with, and no matter what branch of science he enters, he is working with God's book. When he takes up his scientific labors, he opens God's book. Figuratively speaking, as he conducts his scientific investigations and searches out the secrets of the universe, he is paging through God's book of nature, perusing it, delving into its details, and studying it carefully. Whether he admits this or not makes absolutely no difference as to the fact. The unbelieving scientist will never admit that when he labors in his particular branch of science, he is working with God's book. Nevertheless, he is reading that book, whether he acknowledges the author of that book or not, and whether he has spiritual eyes to discern the real contents of that book or not. He cannot avoid this.

This is the plain teaching of scripture.

Romans 1 is an important passage because it applies not only to the scientist, but also to mankind in general, and verses 18–20 speak to the matter under discussion. The apostle in verse 18 mentions the wrath of God that is revealed from heaven against all ungodliness and unrighteousness of men, who hold the truth in unrighteousness. Concerning these men Paul writes, "That which may be known of God is manifest in them; for God hath shewed it unto them" (v. 19). What can be known of God is manifest not merely *to* them, but *in* them. The reason for this is that God himself has showed it to them. Hence no man can escape this knowledge of God. The apostle goes on to explain how God shows this to them: "For the invisible things of him from the creation of the world are clearly seen" (v. 20). How can this be? The text explains: "being understood by the things that are made," meaning creation, the universe, the works of God's hands. What can be clearly seen? The text answers: "his eternal power and Godhead" (v. 20). This is scripture's testimony about the things with which every natural scientist necessarily labors. He comes face-to-face with the testimony of God's eternal power and Godhead. This is true whether or not the scientist admits this.

God takes care that every man, the unbeliever as well as the believer, has sufficient natural light, natural understanding, and power of intellect to read the book of creation, and not only to read it, but also to read it intelligently and to interpret it: "The invisible things of [God] from the creation of the world are *clearly seen*, being understood by the things that are made" (Rom. 1:20). This means that as far as that book is concerned and as far as man's power of mind and intellect is concerned, he can clearly see God's eternal power and Godhead in that book of nature or creation. This is a scriptural fact. The man who reads that book of God is held responsible; he must give an answer for what he reads. Romans 1:20 tells us that this is the purpose and the result: "so that they are without excuse." Hence man is left in the position that he can give an answer and that he must give an answer. And that answer ought to be that he acknowledges God's eternal power and Godhead, and that he knows God and glorifies and thanks him as God.

Additionally, the modern scientist and modern man in general have much more than this book of creation, for man lives in the nominally Christian world, and in that nominally Christian world he has the Bible. In the Bible the truth concerning the origin and the nature of the entire world with which the scientist labors is set forth, so that he is still more emphatically left without excuse.

I want to emphasize that the scientist works with God's book of creation because there is no disharmony between God's testimony of himself as the Creator in the works of his hands and his testimony in scripture of himself as the Creator. One and the same God is revealed in his twofold revelation. I also want to emphasize that the scientist is always confronted by the necessity of giving a spiritual, ethical answer.

The Evolutionist and God's Book of Creation

What happens when the unbelieving, ungodly, evolutionistic scientist reads God's book of creation?

I do not say, when the *scientist* reads that book, but, when the *unbelieving, evolutionistic scientist* reads that book. We cannot lump all scientists together. There is a spiritual difference. From a spiritual viewpoint every scientist begins with either the bias of faith or the bias of unbelief, and if he is consistent, he builds the entire structure of his science from that bias.

What does the ungodly, unbelieving, evolutionistic scientist do with God's book?

He can read it, and he can see not only scientific facts and data, but he can also read things in that book about God. The scientist gathers data concerning the universe. He classifies and interprets that data, and following that interpretation, he comes to a conclusion. And his conclusion is the exact opposite of what that book tells him. His conclusion is, "There is no God. There is no Creator. Things came of themselves, or things had no beginning. But there is no creator God."

That is a spiritual conclusion. The reading and interpretation of God's book of creation are spiritual matters, and the ungodly scientist's conclusion is not due to an intellectual lack. It is not due to his inability to read. He has his remnants of natural light, but the light that is in him is spiritual darkness. Because he is spiritually darkness, the ungodly scientist does not want God, and because he does not want God, he rules God out of his own book. The Lord Jesus says that if the light that is in a man is darkness, how great is that darkness! (Matt. 6:23). The

Canons of Dordt, in speaking about man's glimmerings of natural light, teach:

> So far is this light of nature from being sufficient to bring him to a saving knowledge of God, and to true conversion, that he is incapable of using it aright even in things natural and civil. Nay farther, this light, such as it is, man in various ways renders wholly polluted, and holds it [back] in unrighteousness; by doing which he becomes inexcusable before God.[1]

Such is the correct evaluation of unbelieving science and its conclusions from a scriptural and Reformed viewpoint. This should be the evaluation that we as children of God maintain not concerning science, but concerning unbelieving science.

The practical significance of this is that as Christians we must not gullibly accept all that is presented in the name of science in this scientific age. We must evaluate critically and with spiritual discernment.

---

1 Canons of Dordt 3–4.4, in ibid., 3:588.

The Science
of the Theistic Evolutionist

We are more directly concerned with the science and the alleged scientific conclusions of the theistic evolutionist.

Commonly these scientists, generally classified as Christians, make one sad mistake: they compromise with the science of the unbelieving, evolutionistic scientist who rules God out of his own book. Not only do they compromise materially with regard to their teachings, with the result that they present an essentially contradictory mixture of evolutionism and theism, but behind the compromise in their teachings is also a mistaken but fundamental compromise in their method.

The Christian scientist is bound to recognize the truth of God's twofold revelation in scripture and in the works of his hands. He is also bound to the principle that God's revelation is essentially one, and that therefore there can be no contradiction in that twofold revelation.

But the theistic evolutionist in his science fails to distinguish between the data of the book of creation (in which God spells his name in his creation) and the unbelieving interpretation and method of interpretation of that data that the evolutionist follows. As a result, he follows the evolutionist all the way in his interpretation, until he comes to his conclusion. But as a Christian, he cannot accept the evolutionist's conclusion, for at the point of that conclusion he confronts scripture and his theistic faith. Then he is bound to say, "No, I don't want the conclusion that there is no God. I don't want to get rid of God." The result is the essentially contradictory teaching of theistic evolutionism.

What has happened to the theistic evolutionist's method of science not from a formally scientific, but from a biblical viewpoint? In one form or other, he says that we must take God's revelation in his book of creation and his revelation in scripture side by side. Put in this form, that sounds rather innocent. But as a matter of practice, as well as principle, he ends by adjusting the scriptures to the supposedly scientific conclusions that he has read or that others have read to him out of the book of creation. Here is the core of the whole problem; and it is at this point that the fundamental mistake is made, a mistake that is theological in its nature. That error has to do with the relation between God's revelation in nature (with which science deals directly) and God's revelation in scripture.

Numerous examples that illustrate this error can be produced. A concrete illustration is found in a book by John De Vries.

> The Christian recognizes that there are two documents, with regard to the formation of the universe and its inhabitants, at his disposal. The first, and most important, of these is the Bible, which comes to us with the authority of its sacred inspiration. This revelation fitly opens with a brief account of the creation of the material world, animated nature and man himself. Side by side, we have another manifestation of the same divine mind, the book of nature, itself the work of God, which is open to our curious gaze. To man alone, among all created beings, has been granted the privilege of reading in it. This he does by patient and intelligent researches. Both these books are legitimate sources of knowledge, but we must

learn to read them aright. We should not hope to gain, much less ask, from science the knowledge it can never give, nor seek from the Bible, the science which it does not intend to teach. As the opening chapter of this volume seeks to demonstrate, we should receive from the Bible, on faith, the fundamental truths to which science cannot attain. The results of scientific research must serve as a running commentary to help us to correctly understand the comprehensive statements of the Biblical account. Only in this way can we truly see that the two books, given to us by the same Author, do not oppose, but complete each other. Together they form the whole revelation of God to man.[2]

Apart from other doubtful elements in the above quotation, there is one statement that is altogether erroneous: "The results of scientific research must serve as a running commentary to help us to correctly understand the

2 John De Vries, *Beyond the Atom* (Grand Rapids, MI: William B. Eerdmans Publishing Company, 1950), 37–38.

comprehensive statements of the Biblical account." Put in plain language, this statement means that science—what we read out of the book of creation and what we derive by way of interpretation of that book of nature—must explain the Bible. Scientific theories and conclusions must rule scriptural exegesis. The book of God in creation must interpret the book of God in scripture. This method is exactly a case of putting the cart in front of the horse. At its root it is a denial of the sole authority of scripture. This is an error that is commonly committed in defining the relation between scripture and science, especially with regard to the subject of creation and the age of the universe.

The disquieting result of this erroneous method is that the plain teaching of Genesis, which ought to be normative for Christian science, is set aside or twisted to make Genesis conform to what science wants it to say. That twisted version of Genesis is then presented as a matter of legitimate interpretation.

Today there are those, also in the Reformed community, who carry this method far. There are those who accommodate themselves wholly to evolutionistic theories and who make an altogether absurd attempt to accommodate

Genesis and its creation record to these theories. Jan Lever (1922–2010), a zoologist at the Free University of Amsterdam, is guilty of this. Not only does he place the first man far back in the dim reaches of prehistory, but he also holds that it is exegetically proper to teach that some prehuman animal became human, and that that man was Adam. In a recent book[3] Johannes Stellingwerf does not hesitate to teach that Adam was not the first man. Both at home and abroad, both among scientists and theologians, the individual who maintains a strict attitude of no compromise with evolutionism or theistic evolutionism and who insists on the literal creation doctrine is becoming increasingly rare. The tendency to subject scripture to science and to substitute theistic evolutionism for the creation doctrine is becoming stronger and stronger and steadily more radical, so that eventually any similarity between these scientific conclusions and Genesis, and between the supposed interpretation of Genesis and the plain language of the book of Genesis, becomes strictly coincidental.

---

3 J. Stellingwerf, *Oorsprong en Toekomst van de Creatieve Mens* [Origin and future of the creative man] (Amsterdam: Buijten and Schipperheijn, 1966).

Against this fundamentally wrong approach and this basically low evaluation of holy scripture I warn the reader. This is probably the most serious aspect of the discarding of the creation doctrine in this age of science. Eventually the following of this rationalistic method and approach will lead to the discarding of all of the miracles and all of scripture. Such is also the lesson of church history. Many individuals and churches have trodden that path before. Let the church take warning!

From a spiritual, ethical viewpoint, the wrong in this approach is that it constitutes an attempted compromise between light and darkness, between faith and unbelief, between revealed truth and human philosophy, between the church and the world. And the two simply will not mix. Unbelief and faith, also in the sphere of science, are antithetical to each other. It is high time that Christian scientists recognize this and act on it resolutely.

The Proper Approach of Faith

Having engaged in lengthy negative criticism with respect to the relation between Genesis and science, I now present the positive and proper approach. It is very simple.

The Christian begins and ends on the basis of the absolute authority of scripture. That is so simple that many scientists would probably call it simplistic. That does not worry me, because I want to maintain the absolute authority of Holy Writ. What worries me is my tendency not to maintain that authority.

One does not have to view scripture as a science textbook to maintain this position. Everyone knows that the Bible is not a science textbook. It does not speak scientific language, and it does not present a scientific analysis of things. When it records the creative work, it does not do so from the viewpoint of an astronomer and his telescope, but from the viewpoint of the earth as the habitation of man and as the center and stage of all history. I am afraid, however, that the fact that there are some who teach or are compelled by their view to maintain that the Bible is a science textbook is an attempt to ridicule adherence to the authority of scripture and its creation record and to reduce that position to absurdity. But it is a poor attempt. The question is not whether the Bible is a science textbook, but whether the Bible records facts and speaks accurately. This must certainly be maintained at all costs.

Concerning the interpretation of the data of the universe, the origin of things and the manner of their origin, and the destiny of things (inextricably bound up in the evolutionary theory), scripture speaks, and scripture speaks inerrantly. Science must bow to that speech of scripture, or it is not true science.

This means that the method of the believing scientist is to interpret God's book of creation by faith in the light of holy scripture. He does not come with his science to scripture and, discovering that the two apparently do not agree, say to himself, "Well, I have to adjust my interpretation of scripture to fit my science and my scientific data." He comes with his science to scripture, and he is willing to bow before the scriptures with his science. And if there is apparent disharmony between the two, he says, "I will have to reexamine and adjust my science and scientific conclusions so they are in harmony with scripture."

That fundamental principle may never be violated. You may not say, "Put science and scripture side by side and treat them equally." That is not Reformed, and it is not in harmony with the principle of scripture's authority.

In the Reformed faith, the faith of the scriptures, there is nothing of equal authority with the scriptures. Such is the language of the Belgic Confession:

> Neither may we compare any writings of men, though ever so holy, with those divine Scriptures; nor ought we to compare custom, or the great multitude, or antiquity, or succession of times or persons, or councils, decrees, or statutes, with the truth of God, for the truth is above all: for all men are of themselves liars, and more vain than vanity itself.[4]

The Christian should keep his Christian perspective in this age of science. We live in an age that is widely characterized as the "age of science," and worldly science is full of vainglory and the pride of life, especially in this space age. The world boasts that there are practically no limits to what science can accomplish. The Christian should remember, however, even apart from the truth that

---

4 Belgic Confession 7, in Schaff, *Creeds of Christendom*, 3:388.

the natural man holds his natural light in unrighteousness, that fallen man has only remnants or glimmerings of natural light. His ability to probe into the book of the universe is very limited. In spite of all his boasting, the great, self-exalted modern man is but a very puny and limited creature. Knowing this, the Christian must beware that he does not idolize science.

Alleged Scientific Evidences

Having discussed the basic principles and the methods, we turn to the subject of the scientific data and alleged scientific evidences, or proofs, that are brought against the literal creation doctrine and that are frequently claimed to make the maintenance of the literal creation doctrine utterly foolish and impossible. Undoubtedly it is this aspect of our subject in which there is the most popular interest, even though it is not the most fundamental aspect of the subject. Undoubtedly there are also many people of God who are dazzled by these claims from scientific quarters and who are awed by what is claimed to be and what may superficially seem to be overwhelming and foolproof evidence. From this viewpoint it will be fruitful to consider these claims of scientists.

There are various kinds of data and alleged proofs against the literal creation doctrine and in favor of evolutionism that have arisen from several closely related sciences.

First, there is the science called historical geology. It is inaccurate to speak of it simply as geology, for geology is a legitimate science that enters into many other areas. Historical geology is the study of the rock strata, the layers of rock scattered all over the world of God's creation. On the basis of that study, the historical geologist sets up a geological column in which he claims the various layers of rock are placed in proper historical order as they were deposited in time. However, there is no such thing anywhere in the world as a geological column. That column is theoretical; it is an idea. Nowhere can you find all of the strata that are supposed to be in the geological column and in the fixed order theoretically assigned to them. In fact, the geologist claims that if every layer were given its theoretical maximum size, and if all the layers were piled up on one another, there would be a column a hundred miles deep. But that column is not found anywhere in creation. Moreover, in connection with that geological column there is a time scale set up, which goes back billions of years.

Second, there is a science called paleontology. This science studies fossils in conjunction with historical geology and with a view to establishing various ages in history and prehistory, as it is called, back into those dim billions of years. This study is supposed to show an evolution in the realm of the living creature. And the paleontologist concludes and establishes from this study of fossils an evolution in the rock strata.

Third, there is anthropology, the study of man's evolution. Anthropology is concerned particularly with the ancient forebears of modern man, with prehistoric man and various supposed specimens of prehistoric man. Prehistoric men are supposed to have lived in various parts of the world hundreds of thousands and even millions of years ago.

Fourth, the science of historical archeology must also be mentioned. Archeology busies itself with finding and digging up remnants and evidences of past civilizations, and it is a legitimate study. Historical archeology is interested in finding evidences of ancient civilizations and producing proofs or indications of human civilizations as far back as possible, beyond any limits of recorded history, and especially beyond the commonly acknowledged limits of biblical history.

Fifth, there is the science of astronomy, the study of the heavenly luminaries. In connection with our subject, astronomy is used in reasoning from the claimed distances of the heavenly lights and the time that it requires for light to travel, in order to make a mathematical computation of how long it would have taken light to reach our earth from a given distant star, and thus to draw conclusions as to the age of the world.

In connection with the above scientific studies, especially in recent times, a great appeal is made to various methods of radioactive dating. Especially because of these dating methods the evidences produced by science are alleged to be virtually unassailable. There have been various attempts at dating the universe before the advent of atomic science and these radioactive dating methods, but this technology is supposed to be very accurate and reliable. I will mention and explain these methods briefly and nontechnically.

Various methods are used to date inorganic, mineral matter. Various chemical elements are radioactive to a certain degree, and they have a tendency to disintegrate into other elements or isotopes. The rate of that disintegration can be measured. If there is a mineral containing both the parent substance and the daughter element, as it is called, science can compute by the process of disintegration the time period during which the daughter element has been accumulating. There are methods that involve the disintegration of uranium and thorium into radium, helium, and lead and the disintegration of rubidium into strontium and potassium into argon and calcium. Recently there has been mention of a method called glass fission track dating.

There is also the carbon 14 method of radiological dating, which is applied to organic materials and which is said to be useful for relatively shorter periods of time—according to some, under sixty thousand years. Wood items, for example, can be dated by this method, which is used especially in the dating of ancient civilizations.

On the basis of all these studies and methods of dating, allegedly highly accurate conclusions are reached.

Today the conclusion is reached that the universe is four and one-half billion years old. The conclusion is also reached that man and civilization of one kind or another are much older than the six to ten thousand years within which the creation doctrine is usually presented.

A Brief Critique of This Alleged Proof

What must the Christian say about this evidence?

The claim is that all this evidence is very scientific and accurate, that it is compelling evidence, that the one who believes in a literal creation in six, twenty-four-hour days cannot escape its force, and that this scientific evidence is the downfall of the creation doctrine, especially of the literal creation doctrine.

What do scientists do with this alleged evidence in relation to scripture?

Obviously the rank evolutionist does not care about scripture. He chooses in favor of his scientific data and his alleged evidence, and he discards anything scripture says. In fact, he mocks the Bible. The evolutionist also discards God's book of creation. Although the book of creation plainly testifies of God, the unbelieving evolutionist denies the testimony of the very data he studies and on which he claims to base his proof. According to scripture all the data point to the eternal power and godhead of the Creator in one way or another. The evolutionist denies this, and he denies God; and he worships and serves the creature rather than the Creator.

In the case of the theistic evolutionist, we face something different, and I am convinced that it is more dangerous and insidious than outright evolutionism. The theistic evolutionist cannot overtly discard scripture and its creation record if he wants to remain a theist. What then is he compelled to do in order to maintain the evolutionism that he alleges his science compels him to believe? He must adjust the Genesis record to fit his science. He believes that his scientific data, which he equates with God's revelation in nature, must serve as a running commentary on scripture, not that scripture must serve as an infallible guide in his scientific investigations. As a result, he makes room in the creation week for four and one-half billion years, and he makes room in the work of creation for a process of evolution or progressive creation.

His method and approach are wrong.

Essentially this is following a rationalistic method, the result of which is contrary to the plain and authoritative teaching of scripture. Science must get its billions of years into scripture's creation week. It does not help to get these long periods of time into history after the week of creation, for according to scripture, all things were finished at the end of that week. But as soon as the theistic evolutionist attempts to introduce four and one-half billion years into the Bible's creation week, he runs squarely into the Bible's testimony that creation took place in six literal, twenty-four-hour days. Into that week his four and one-half billion years simply do not fit. Hence by some exegetical sleight of hand, he must force them to fit. Thus in the name of interpretation, which is not legitimate exegesis whatsoever, he gets rid of the six days and substitutes long periods of evolution. This is not exegesis, but eisegesis, what the Dutch call *inlegkunde*, a laying into the text of scripture something that is not there and that the text does not say. Such is the rationalistic method of adjusting scripture's record to make room for these alleged scientific conclusions.

The conclusion to which the Christian scientist should come to is exactly the opposite. If his science leads him to conclusions that are plainly contrary to scripture's testimony concerning the creation of all things and the age of the universe, he should discard his conclusions as being impossible. That is not being unscientific; it is responsible Christian science. The Christian scientist should reexamine his scientific data in the light of scripture, in order to discover, if possible, the correct way of harmonizing his data and evidence with scripture. But even if and when it should prove impossible for him to harmonize his scientific data with the testimony of scripture, he must allow scripture to stand, and he must take the position that somewhere along the line his scientific investigations have been faulty.

In close connection with this subject is the biblical chronology after creation. The ideas of secular history have crept into Christian thinking, with the result that a place must be found in the Christian conception for a prehistory and for prehistoric civilizations, while scripture furnishes only history from the beginning of the world. The relatively brief chronology that the Bible presents is often mocked as ridiculously impossible. It is claimed that the generations of Adam in Genesis 5 and the generations of Shem in Genesis 11 furnish nothing in the way of a chronology. It is asserted that the Bible is not interested in chronology. This is true in terms of mere telling of time, but it is not true regarding chronology's intimate connection with revelation and history's inseparable connection with time. It is also claimed that there are any number of untold generations that have been omitted in the records of Genesis. However, on an exegetical basis the biblical chronology cannot be lightly waved aside, and on biblical grounds it is difficult to disprove a definite chronology of the prediluvian and immediate postdiluvian periods. Biblical grounds must be adduced, and if on biblical grounds that chronology is stretched to the utmost, the age of the world is about ten thousand years.

For many reasons I prefer to hold a much stricter view than that.

From a practical viewpoint, what is the Christian to think of science's alleged evidences?

I wish to make some observations as to the reliability of this alleged evidence. Although the attitude is frequently taken that it is preposterous to challenge this evidence, the fact is that the methods of science have changed many, many times, even in recent years. In my research on this subject I read somewhere that there have been over forty methods that have been tried and then discarded in reaching the conclusion that the universe is very old. Science has been very changeable. Science has had to admit that its research has been unreliable. The conclusions that various evolutionistic scientists have reached have also changed. At one time it was thought that the world was fifty-seven million years old. Later Lord Kelvin revised this to twenty to forty million years. Then the estimate was revised to ninety to one hundred million years. After the advent of radiological dating in the mid 1950s, the most accurate conclusion reached on the basis of data at that time was that the world was two billion years old. Today many claim that the universe is four and a half billion years old; some make the figure three billion plus; others say it should be five billion plus. These changeable conclusions certainly cast unfavorable reflections on their reliability. One is moved to ask, what *does* science want? The same is true with respect to the history of man. Estimates of his age made via the carbon 14 method range from thirty-five thousand to seventy thousand years.

All these figures are quite unimaginable. Perhaps science can find a certain amount of safety in these dim and unimaginable billions. But do you know what six thousand years is in relation to four and a half billion years? It is comparable to one-tenth of one second in relation to a whole day. But that is supposed to be the relation between history and prehistory. This whole conception is silly from the viewpoint of divine wisdom. It is worse than building a two-stall garage on the foundation of a skyscraper.

These claims of science can also be criticized from a scientific viewpoint. I will leave that to scientists, who are much more capable of this than a nonscientist such as I. Scientists themselves have frequently pointed out that these evidences are not as cut and dried as they have been presented to be. There have been red faces when living specimens of animals that were supposedly long extinct and prehistoric have been produced to contradict fossil evidence. Nor are scientists unanimous on the subject of the dating methods. There is not only contradictory evidence, but there are also arguments that can be raised solely on a scientific basis. For example, it can be argued that a fundamental law of science is the conservation of matter, while the evolutionist needs the creation, the formation of *new* matter. Another fundamental law of all science is the universal tendency toward disorder, disintegration, and decay, while evolutionism needs advancement, development, and progress.

Above all, the entire evolutionistic presentation, whether of the nontheist or the theist, comes into conflict with scripture's testimony. On that basis alone it may not be countenanced by the Christian.

Positive Suggestions toward a Proper Christian View

We can legitimately ask whether there are no biblical answers and positive solutions to some of the problems and apparent conflicts between scientific research and the testimony of Genesis. My answer is that there are such solutions, and I wish to make a few suggestions of such a positive nature.

Before I do this, I must point out the error inherent in much scientific thinking with respect to our subject, an error into which the Christian scientist must not fall. I refer to what is called *uniformitarianism*. What is it?

> Uniformitarianism is the belief that existing physical processes, acting essentially as at present, are sufficient to account for all past changes and for the present state of the astronomic, geologic, and biologic universe. The principle of uniformity in *present* processes is both scientific and scriptural (Gen. 8:22), but comes into conflict with biblical revelation when utilized to deny the possibility of *past* or *future* miraculous suspension or alteration of those processes by their Creator.[5]

Uniformitarianism is the hypothesis that all geologic processes and all of the processes involved in radiological dating have always occurred at the same exact rate for four

---

5 John C. Whitcomb, Jr. and Henry M. Morris, *The Genesis Flood* (Grand Rapids, MI: Baker Book House, 1961), 20.

and a half billion years, so that they can be accurately measured and the age of things can be calculated on this basis. But what is it spiritually and theologically in the light of scripture? It is the doctrine and the language of the scoffers mentioned in 2 Peter 3:3–4: "All things continue as they were from the beginning of the creation."

Not only can this hypothesis of uniformitarianism not be proved scientifically and on the basis of the definition of science cited in the early part of this chapter, but the entire theory cannot stand in the light of scripture. Scripture's truth is that things definitely have not continued as they were from the beginning.

Against this background I present a few positive suggestions.

First, scripture presents in the creation narrative the picture of what can be called a full-grown creation, and therefore the picture of a creation with the appearance of age. When God made Adam, he did not make a baby or a baby in the womb who was yet to reach maturity. He created a man and a woman who were full-grown on the day of their creation. When God called the animals into existence, he did not bring them into existence through eggs, much less through a long evolutionary process. He called them out of the waters and out of the earth, and they stood there, mature and complete. When God formed the world of plants, he did not plant seeds. On the contrary, the chicken is before the egg, and the tree is before the seed. The same is true of the entire creation, inorganic as well as organic. Therefore creation had the appearance of age when it was formed. Some people have said, "In that case God lies; he deceives men, and he fools science." No, God cannot lie, and he does not lie. He has plainly revealed his creative work, and he tells us what kind of creation he made. Man is the liar, not God.

Second, science does not and cannot study the creation as it was originally formed. The universe we study today is a universe radically changed at the time of the fall and through the curse. There are many indications of this in scripture, and science should pay attention to the changes scripture points out. There was a drastic change in the domain of the animals at the time of the fall. There was also a change in man's dominion over the animals. There was a change in the earth, which was cursed, and there was a change in the food of man. According to Romans

8:20–2I, the whole creation came under the bondage of corruption through the fall and the curse. Here is an area to be considered by Christian science.

Third, there was a radically different world before the flood than after the flood. That is scripture's literal testimony in 2 Peter 3:5–6: "For this they willingly are ignorant of, that by the word of God the heavens were of old, and the earth standing out of the water and in the water: Whereby the world that then was, being overflowed with water, perished." That is clear and strong language—not scientific language, but very clear and strong: "The world that *then* was perished." There is such a difference between our world and the prediluvian world that the Bible speaks of it as another world. That past world was destroyed by the flood, by a destruction that was comparable to and typical of the final catastrophic destruction of the world. We live in the world that *now is*, not in the world that *then was*, and there are many scripturally noted differences between our world and that one. According to 2 Peter 3, one of the most fundamental differences is that the former world stood in the water and out of the water. That world stood as close to the water as our world stands to the fire. The heavens and the earth that are now are reserved unto fire. Let Christian science study these differences.

In close connection herewith is the flood itself. Many scientists—and to their shame, many theologians—continually criticize the biblical presentation of the flood. They pick it apart and find all kinds of rationalistic grounds for the impossibility of the flood, for the impossibility of its universality, and for the impossibility of the ark. Biblically conceived, the flood was in every way a tremendous catastrophe, an awful divine intervention, and at the same time a miracle, a wonder of grace. It was miraculous and catastrophic. It was the outpouring of the wrath of God on a wicked world. Unbelieving science has great difficulty with the miraculous, but scripture points to this catastrophe in many ways, as well as to the changes that took place at that time. Consider only the scriptural fact that according to Genesis 7:11 "The fountains of the great deep were broken up, and the windows of heaven were opened." That flood was no ordinary but extraordinarily long rain. Let Christian science consider in the light of scripture the changes wrought in the universe at the time of the flood.

Accept the truth of the flood, and what becomes of uniformitarianism? Accept the testimony of scripture, and consider whether you can even imagine what effects the tremendous pressures of the waters of the flood had upon the earth in comparison with the devastation that a small local flood can wreak today. Then left out of the picture is the biblical account of the flood as a catastrophic and violent upheaval.

There have been more changes. There was a direct intervention in the life span of mankind after the flood. There was another such intervention in society and civilization at the time of Babel.

These biblical materials must be used positively by the Christian scientist for developing his views and his answers to evolutionism along biblical lines. Very little of this has been done in the past. A much maligned and belittled but notable work has been accomplished in this respect by Henry Morris in the book *The Genesis Flood*. I commend that work, even though I may not agree with all that is written in it. In general, Christians have had a kind of inferiority complex. They have been afraid to oppose the claims of unbelieving science. They have been afraid to strike out on their own and to develop their own scientific theories and explanations in this area. They have been too much on the defensive and too ready to compromise and to capitulate to worldly science.

Finally, let me sound a warning. Let us beware that we do not allow these current theories to find their way into our homes, grade schools, high schools, and into our churches. To the extent that they have already gained entrance, let us resolutely root them out. I have earlier remarked that men are becoming increasingly bold and radical in promulgating these views and in trying to make a place for themselves even in conservative and Reformed circles. Genesis I–II has been completely discarded by those who have twisted scripture. Next, everything miraculous will be discarded, and finally there will be nothing left of God's word. That is the principle here, and principles work through.

Especially since we live in the last days mentioned in 2 Peter 3, let us stand fast and hold fast what we have, for the sake of the cause of Christ and of the church, for the sake of our own faith, and for the sake of our children.